AUTHORS **BART LOOTSMA AND DICK RIJKEN**
COMMENTS: BRUNO FELIX, MICHAEL HENSEL, BART LOOTSMA, GREG LYNN, WINY MAAS
BERT MULDER, DICK RIJKEN, LARS SPUYBROEK, PHILIPPE WEGNER, NICK WEST

▏▎▍▌▌MEDIA ᴬⁿᵈ ARCHITECTURE▌▌▍▎▏

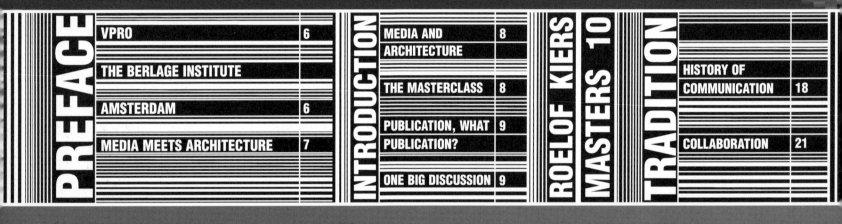

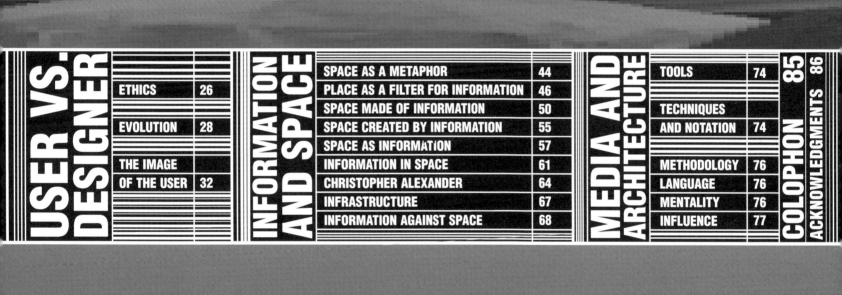

||||||||PREFACE|||| ||| | ||| | | | | | | | | |

IN 1997, THE VPRO AND THE BERLAGE INSTITUTE AMSTERDAM ORGANISED THE FIRST ROELOF KIERS MASTERCLASS ON MEDIA AND ARCHITECTURE

VPRO

The VPRO is a broadcasting organization that produces television and radio programs, as well as a weekly TV guide. The VPRO tries to surprise it's audience with unusual and controversial programs, observing society in an analytical way without prejudice. Creative and journalistic autonomy reign. This approach has enabled the VPRO to develop an explicit style. Much attention goes to informative and cultural programs, where 'open' formats like interviews, documentaries and debates match the VPRO mentality. There are loyal supporters as well as fierce opponents, and lots of healthy discussions. It is becoming apparent that new developments in information technology are beginning to play an increasingly important role in the media industry as a whole. In 1994, the VPRO founded a department for research and development in the field of digital media, aptly named "VPRO Digitaal". VPRO Digitaal investigates the impact of digital technology on society, and its consequences on a broadcasting organization. The department does so by developing (experimental) communication products and services, thereby feeding the organization with food for thought about its future. Since 1994, the department has produced two CD-Roms, a series of successive versions of the VPRO website (www.vpro.nl, forever "new and improved"), and an on-line movie database that allows its users to configure an e-mail service that informs them about films on TV which match

their personal preferences (cinema.vpro.nl). The department (just like the VPRO itself) has gained a reputation as an innovative and challenging player in its field, always at the cutting edge where content meets technology. The department highly values its relationships with various kinds of educational institutions, which form an important part of the motivation for organizing this Masterclass.

THE BERLAGE INSTITUTE AMSTERDAM

The Berlage Institute Amsterdam is a Postgraduate Laboratory of Architecture. With the founding of the BiA in 1990, the Netherlands acquired a forum where contemporary urban issues can be discussed and where a dialogue can take place between architects and interested people from different disciplines. The fact that the Institute, with its strong international profile, is located in the Netherlands means that it is not only the cultural implications of the Dutch architectural tradition which can make an important contribution, but also Dutch achievements in the fields of art, civil engineering, literature and media. This cultural embedding means that the Institute is open on the one hand to both Dutch and international fields of interest, while on the other hand maintaining its profile as an independent centre for research. In the centre of the research interest are architecture, urban planning and landscape architecture as well as other tangential but influential disciplines. The interdisciplinary attitude within research has been adopted on the grounds that architecture can not be seen as an independent discipline, but as simply one element in an increasingly complex society. The open forum

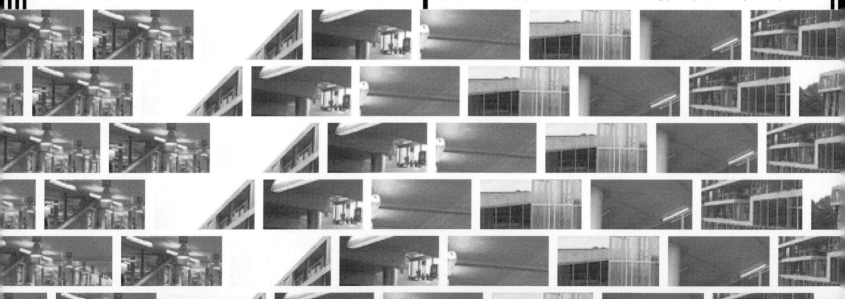

which the Institute aims to be is benefiting students and professors alike, as each individual student is encouraged to extend his or her individual capacities and interests. This means that within the Institute students are enabled to develop the strategies they need to maintain continuing professional responsibility and creativity. The BiA has been organising Masterclasses since its very beginning. For a Masterclass a renowned architect or architectural theoretician is invited to be a "Master". This Master formulates an assignment, a brief, and invites a number of guest professors who are known to have interest in and affinity with the chosen subject or approach. At least three Masterclasses are held each year. A Masterclass provides a good opportunity for generating ideas and allowing experiments about new and urgent, as yet unsolved issues in the field of architecture, urban planning, art, media and technology. The Masterclasses are also open to participants who are not students of the Institute.

MEDIA MEETS ARCHITECTURE

In June of 1997, the VPRO, formerly located in thirteen separate buildings throughout Hilversum (a city that is home to most of the Dutch broadcasting industry), moved to a single new building, designed by MVRDV (Winy Maas, Nathalie de Vries, Jacob van Rijs). For the first time in its history, all of the VPRO's departments are now together under one roof. This greatly affects the way in which people work together and communicate with each other. While the move into the new building was being anticipated in 1996, it was the talk of the town in all of the old villas. At that time, VPRO Digitaal

was developing an internal media infrastructure that addressed issues of collaboration in the context of media production. This prompted a discussion about the similarities and differences between media design and architecture. If both disciplines address similar issues, such as processes of collaboration or the establishment of identity, shouldn't they work together more than they currently do in common practice? The Berlage Institute Amsterdam became involved in the discussion, and soon the idea for a joint Masterclass, one involving media designers and architects, was born to further investigate these issues. Where are you when you are engaged in a conversation using a mobile phone on a train? Processes of communication are no longer connected to fixed places and moments. They alter our sense of "where we are" and "who we are". How will the new forms of electronic communication affect the spatial relationships in design, architecture and urbanism? Conversely, how are the media's messages dependent on architectural space? And most of all, what does this mean for the individual, the group, the organization, as producers or users of information or space? These issues are central to both the VPRO and the Berlage Institute Amsterdam. We decided to investigate them in this Masterclass, hoping to find inspiration and promising new territories for both of us.

We hope that this publication will inspire readers as much as the Masterclass itself inspired us. In order to reach a wide audience, we have decided to publish it in the English language. Enjoy!

WIEL ARETS, BRUNO FELIX.

INTRODUCTION

MEDIA AND ARCHITECTURE

In our Western cultures, we are in the transition from an industrial to an information society. This transition is not just a matter of technology — it is also (and, in the end, mainly) a social and a cultural event. Design is where technology meets culture. The disciplines of both architecture and media design are constantly rethinking and transforming themselves. The impact of information and communication technologies on our culture is a shared concern. Can architecture answer questions that emerge in media design, and vice versa? Can the dialogue between these disciplines inspire a truly integrative approach? Do we need a new design discipline? Can we design buildings that tell stories, or media that create spaces? We decided to bring together some of the best people in these disciplines and invited them to play with ideas in a Masterclass setting.

THE MASTERCLASS

The Masterclass consisted of two events at the Berlage Institute Amsterdam: one week of work in February, 1997 and one week in April, 1997. There were four teams of masters, who coached four groups of participants (architecture students from the Berlage Institute Amsterdam and various kinds of media design students from a number of Dutch design academies). The master teams each consisted of a media designer and an architect: Philippe Wegner and Greg Lynn; Bert Mulder and Lars Spuybroek; Nick West and Michael Hensel; and Bruno Felix, Dick Rijken and Winy Maas.

The first week was devoted to clarifying the field of possibilities. What are the issues? What are the design dimensions? Where do the different design disciplines intersect? These questions were to be considered, on one hand, in the context of the interaction between the VPRO and its staff, and on the other hand between the VPRO and its audience. The role of the new building within all of this was be considered as well, related to current and projected developments in the media industry. During this week, there was an excursion to the site of the new VPRO building, the masters gave public presentations about their work, and all of the groups presented the results of their research at the end of the week. The second week focused on production, with all groups working towards designs and design ideas that were also presented at the end of the week.

PUBLICATION, WHAT PUBLICATION?

As the Masterclass progressed, it became apparent to everyone involved that there was a wealth of fascinating and challenging issues behind the questions that we started with. Both disciplines enjoyed the wealth of knowledge and experience that "the other side" provided. But there were heated debates as well, some based on misunderstandings, and others fueled by strong disagreements. Inspiration and confusion went hand in hand. The presentations of the results showed enormous diversity, ranging from methodological issues, specific designs related to the VPRO, all the way to new proposals for the structure of the building industry. The amount of energy generated was enormous. Many presentations were

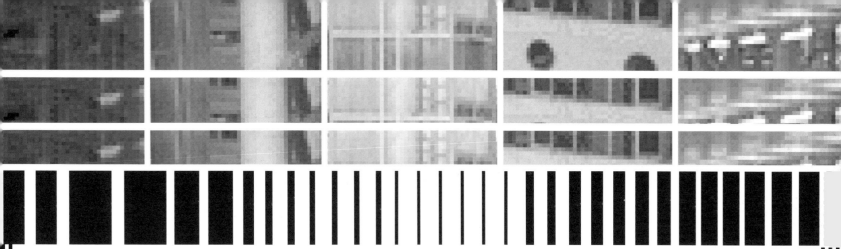

true performances, fully utilizing both the available media as well as people. All this made the promise which we had made to make a publication based on the Masterclass a frightening prospect. There was simply no way to capture the depth and richness of all the work in any kind of written form, and we found the idea of selecting projects based on the availability of printable outcomes downright silly. So we didn't even try, and started looking for an alternative approach...

Because the Masterclass had strengthened our belief in the importance of connecting the disciplines, but also our suspicions about the complexity of the interactions between them, we decided to devote the publication to a more general discussion, rather than try and untangle all the specific results. Bart Lootsma (architecture critic, connected to the Berlage Institute Amsterdam) and Dick Rijken (media designer, connected to the VPRO), two of the instigators of the project, agreed to engage in an e-mail discussion about the interaction between the two disciplines.

ONE BIG DISCUSSION
And so it happened. We decided that the discussion was to become an introductory debate; an experienced professional in one field can be a student in another. An e-mail message that addressed an issue would generate a response, and then a response to the response, and so forth. E-mail is an informal medium and, as you will see, so is the discussion. At times, everyone would lose track of who had said what, but the discussion came alive through frank attempts at probing the other's views on the issues

raised. It led to many misunderstandings, many disagreements, lots of fun, and many questions which still remain unanswered. Afterwards, the entire discussion was mailed to the other masters, who were then asked for their comments on the document. The result is what you now have before you. Is architecture a conservative discipline, stuck in its old ways? Are media designers obsessed with the individual? Why do architects constantly talk about "transgression" without being able to explain to media designers what the word means (and most of them are still in the dark)? Are digital media truly "new" media? Are media designers post-hippie idealists, blind to the marvelous insights of post-post-modern thinkers? Can architects and media designers work together because they create their pictures in the same digital domain, or because they worship the same ideals? Is talking about architecture more important for architects than designing buildings? Are media designers making mistakes that architects have long ago learned to avoid? Why are architects so scared of thinking about specific situations and people? Do media designers really want people to look like Robocop?

In the end, all of this is about collaboration, about communication, about two disciplines trying to make sense of one another. We hope that this discussion will lead to many other discussions, and that it's only the beginning. The questions outnumber the answers, but we hope that you will find them useful and inspiring. And that if you are thinking of getting involved in this field, they can help you get started...

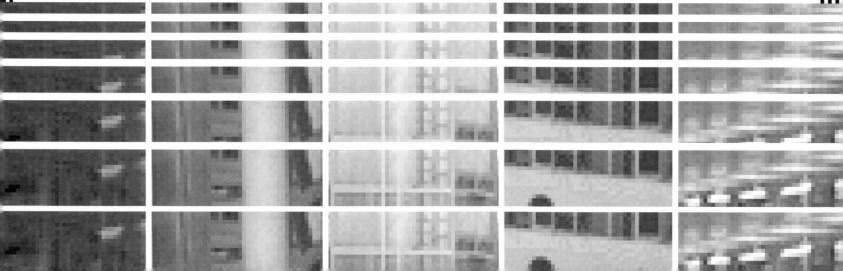

ROELOF KIERS

ROELOF KIERS, WHO JOINED THE VPRO IN 1969, WAS ONE OF DUTCH TELEVISION'S LEADING DOCUMENTARY MAKERS DURING THE 1970S. AFTER BEING NAMED EDITOR IN CHIEF, HE DEFENDED THE INTERESTS OF VPRO TELEVISION WITH HEART AND SOUL IN THE RAPIDLY CHANGING MEDIA LANDSCAPE. HE RECOGNIZED THE NEW MEDIA'S SIGNIFICANCE FOR PUBLIC BROADCASTING QUITE EARLY ON. UNDER KIERS, VPRO'S DIGITAL DEPARTMENT WAS ESTABLISHED, ITS BRIEF BEING TO INVESTIGATE NEW FORMS OF COMMUNICATION AND MEDIA. ROELOF KIERS DIED IN 1994.

MASTERS

BRUNO FELIX worked as a television director for several cultural productions for local and national broadcasters. From 1992 he worked for the VPRO programs "Prima Vista" and "Roerend Goed". In 1994 he was asked by Roelof Kiers (the former director of the VPRO TV department) to set up "VPRO-digitaal", and a weekly program on new media, called "W.E.B.". As director of VPRO digitaal, a media research department exploring the influence of digital technology on the production, distribution and use of media, he was responsible for the new media strategy of the VPRO. He defined projects ranging from training VPRO employees to prototyping new program formats and developing operational Web-sites. He was the Project Manager for two CD-ROM projects: "The interactive TV guide" and "The virtual debate" an interactive debate with four speakers on safety and threats in the 21 century. He was producer for the event in the ZULU tent at the Lowlands pop festival in 1996: a TV program, a public exhibit, and a web site which covered the festival program in text, video, and audio. He was responsible for the development of numerous experimental web-sites which explore new ways of drama, youth programming and journalism. One of these is the "24 Hour Cinema Service", an online searchable film database with the ability to recommend movies, based on personal profiles and an e-mail service to notify users when movies they might be interested in are broadcasted on Dutch television.

Another website is the Internet radio station "3voor12". Recently, the department developed a tailor-made chatbox with audio and video feedback to use in conjunction with TV and radio programs for on-line games, interviews or guided surf tours.

MICHAEL HENSEL (born 1965) has been an architect in private practice since 1989. He is a co-founder of OCEAN and OCEAN c and currently teaches at the AA in the Diploma School. He has previously taught at the AA Graduate Design program, the Berlage Institute, and the University of Art and Design in Helsinki.

NETWORKING: THE PRACTICE OF INTER-CHANGE. OCEANnet has emerged as one of the most recent forms of architectural practice in the 90s, operating as a transnational collaborative network of architects, designers, urbanists and consultants from various disciplines. Present locations include five European collegiums based in Cologne, Helsinki, London, Ljubljana, Oslo and an American node based in Boston. This new form of collaborative practice is based on the potential of the reconfigurative, "just-in-time" nature of its internal organization and operative logic: design teams are formed around specific design problems for the duration of a project and consist of the core members of the OCEANnet, the collegiums, and affiliated consultants.

TRANSITION AS TASK: UNFOLDING DIVERSITY. OCEANnet's scope of work is located within the fuzzy zone of cross-disciplinary re/search. The task is to promote a radically heuristic modus operandi and to look for new synergetic solutions to design problems in fields as diverse as architecture, urban design, furniture design, landscape design, media design/new media applications, design theory, and re-search in new materials.

BART LOOTSMA (born in Amsterdam, 1957) is an historian, critic and curator in the fields of architecture, design and the visual arts. He earned his degree in Architectural History and Theory from the Eindhoven University of Technology with a reconstruction of the "Poème Électronique", the Philips pavilion at the 1958 Brussels World Fair, designed by Le Corbusier, Xenakis and Varèse. Together with the architectural historian Mariëtte van Stralen, he founded V.O.F. Boiling Phenomena. Bart Lootsma was an editor of "de Architect" and "Forum", and is currently a member of the editorial board of "ARCHIS", "The Architecture Yearbook" in the Netherlands and is the *Herausgeber* of the Berlin-based magazine "Daidalos". He also contributes regularly to "l'Architecture d'Aujourd'hui" and "DOMUS". He was an Assistant Professor and Lecturer at the Meisterklasse für Visuelle Gestaltung at the Hochschule für Künstlerische und Industrielle Gestaltung in Linz (Austria), Head of the Department of 3D design at the Academy of the Arts in Arnhem, and Lecturer at the Eindhoven University of Technology (the Netherlands). He has lectured and taught at the Academies of Architecture of Amsterdam, Rotterdam, Tilburg and Arnhem. He is currently a Guest Professor at the Berlage Institute (Thesis Work) and lectures at the PAS, both of which are postgraduate courses in Amsterdam. Bart Lootsma has published numerous articles and several books and catalogues on architecture, design and the visual arts. He was and remains a member of several Dutch governmental, semi-governmental and municipal committees and juries dealing with architecture, design and the visual arts. He had shows of his own work (installations and photography) in Holland, Austria and the USA, and has curated and co-curated exhibitions for, among others, the University of Technology in Eindhoven, the Badischer Kunstverein in Karlsruhe, the Centre Georges Pompidou in Paris and the Kunsthalle in Vienna.

GREG LYNN is an architectural theorist, designer and professor at Columbia University. He studied Philosophy and Environmental Design at Miami University of Ohio and received a Master's degree in Architecture from Princeton University in 1988. He worked as a guest lecturer at Ohio State University and the University of Illinois, Chicago (1991-92), and in Bucharest, Romania, at the Soros Foundation's Summer Workshop in Architecture (1993). Currently he is Adjunct Assistant Professor at Columbia University's Graduate School of Architecture, Planning and Preservation. In the past, Lynn worked for Antoine Predock Architect (1987), and for Eisenman Architects (1987-91). He was also a member of the Design Team at the Frankfurt Biocentrum. Today he mainly works at his own architecture office, "Greg Lynn FORM" (established in 1992), for which he is designing the Citron House in Amagansett, NY.

Lynn has participated in conferences including "AnyWise, An Organism for Living"(Seoul, Korea, in June 1995) and "Beyond the Wall: Architecture, Ideology and Culture in Central and Eastern Europe" (Bucharest, Romania, June-July 1995). His publications include pieces in: "Assemblage 26, The Renewed Novelty of Symmetry: Cardiff Bay Opera House Competition Project" (Cambridge, MA: MIT Press); "El Croquis", Editorial, Ben van Berkel (Madrid, 1995); "ANY Magazine" (New York), Charles Gwathmey, "A Physique out of Proportion", 1995. Over the past three years, the office of Greg Lynn/ FORM has produced projects that challenge traditional ideas about architectural design methods. The work has integrated the computer into its design process in an increasingly innovative manner. Used as a tool to investigate design decisions dynamically through animations and the moving section and to represent the project both in 2D as well as in 3D in Cabrini and Cardiff, the computer then plays a role in the generation of forms in response to programmatic exigencies in the Yokohama project. Finally, in the Port Authority competition, his most recent project, Lynn is modeling forces on the site, using the advanced inverse kinematics capabilities of Alias PowerAnimator. This charting of forces on the site then inflects the design. The office views the incorporation of state-of-the-art hardware and software (SGI Indigo and Indigo Extremes, running Alias, Wavefront and SoftImage, for which grateful acknowledgement is made by Greg Lynn/FORM to Alias and Wavefront for the donation of their software) as a set of tools to investigate architectural performance within the framework of theories based on performance parameters that are only now being theorized in architecture. Greg, as perhaps the leading voice in the development of these theories, is informed by the work of Prigogine, Thom, Bateson, Deleuze, Thompson, Irigaray, Kwinter, et. al.

WINY MAAS (born 1959), Jacob van Rijs (born 1964) and Nathalie de Vries (born 1965) all trained at the Delft Technische Universiteit; Maas also studied landscape design at the RHSLT in Boskoop. Before setting up their office under an acronym based on their names, they worked individually for practices such as Lapeña & Torres in Barcelona, Van Berkel & Bos in Amsterdam, Mecanoo in Delftand, and the Office for Metropolitan Architecture in Rotterdam. In Berlin, they won the European competition for a housing scheme in 1991. The award marked the start-up of their trio, even if this first project never actually materialized. In 1993 they were commissioned to do the new head office of VPRO, a broadcasting organization in Holland, which broadcasts via the public networks. This building, which was inaugurated in early 1997, has gotten them off to a good start. Their research has mainly to do with high-density areas. The title of their first book, "Statics" (1993), which encompasses several of their projects, refers to the idea of what static is in architecture, and to statistics. In fact, statistical data constitute an important focal point in the elaboration of their projects: they see the city as a datascape. Like Oma and Rem Koolhaas, they use a method based on "systematic idealization", a spontaneous over-estimation of whatever is available, a theoretical barrage in the course of which, thanks to retroactive conceptual and ideological interventions, even features of average quality may also be integrated. The demands outlined in various programs, which in certain cases seem impossible to meet, are followed to the letter, as are the complex and stringent Dutch building regulations. This attitude of placing themselves at the extreme limits of constraints and regulations generates architecture and urban design of an astounding differentiation and complexity. MVRDV does not see high-density as a necessary evil, but rather as an opportunity to open up to an awareness of community life. The interlocking and overlapping of dwellings create many new typologies.

BERT MULDER (born 1952) studied psychology, information technology and future sciences at the International University of Lugano. He was the Head of the Computer Department of the Veronica Broadcasting Organization. Thereafter he was a member of the Apple Technology Program, an "advanced technology" program within Europe. He is now the Director of VOTA Consultancy, a consultancy firm in the field of design, modern information systems and (multi)media. He also works with the Institute of Strategic Management. He taught at the Academy of the Arts in Utrecht in the Interaction Design Department, and is currently teaching at the University of Art and Design in Helsinki in the field of possible combinations between information technology and new forms of living and working. He has organized numerous conferences on cross-cultural subjects and future studies. Since August of 1995, he has been an information advisor for the Dutch government's Lower House, with the brief of developing strategies with regard to the use of information for the benefit of the political process within the democracy.

LARS SPUYBROEK is an architect and one of the founders of NOX, a design office that has a truly multi-disciplinary approach towards architecture and design. Over the past few years, NOX has realized, among other projects, "Soft City", a television production for VPRO TV (1993), the NOX Magazine "A, B, C and D" (1992 - 1995), "SoftSite: A Liquid City Generated by Behavior on the Internet" (V2_Organization, 1996), and has projected an integrated design of architecture and an interactive installation onto the facade of the Netherlands Architecture Institute and the water pavilion, called H2O eXPO (for the Dutch Ministry of Transport, Public Works and Water Management, 1997 as well as for the V2_lab in Rotterdam, 1998). He lectures extensively in the Netherlands and abroad, and has been teaching at numerous universities and academies since 1991. Since 1995, Lars Spuybroek has also been the editor of FORUM, a bilingual architectural quarterly .

DICK RIJKEN After serious excursions into computer science and electronic music, Dick Rijken graduated as a psychologist. He was involved in setting up an expertise center for artificial intelligence at the Utrecht School of the Arts, lecturing on various subjects such as knowledge acquisition, knowledge representation, and music technology. After that, he was Head of the Interaction Design Department at the Faculty for Art, Media and Technology. This mainly involved setting up a four-year curriculum in Interaction Design. In 1995, he worked for the Netherlands Design Institute, where he developed a collaborative workspace for workshop participants of the third Doors of Perception conference.

Since 1995 he has been a permanent staff member of the Sandberg Institute's postgraduate course in Design (the Sandberg Institute is connected to the Gerrit Rietveld Academy). Currently, he is also the Managing Director and Strategy Director at TBWA/e-Company, a consultancy for digital communication, and Project Manager at VPRO Digitaal, a department for new media within a Dutch broadcasting organization. His interests focus on the way that new media and information infrastructures can be used to facilitate conversations between organizations and their "clients".

PHILIPPE WEGNER is s a partner in "DC3 Industrial and Interaction Design". DC3 is an unconventional design consultancy firm, combining competence in "classical" industrial design with interaction design. Among DC3's clients are the Dutch government; manufacturers of electronic, medical and other professional equipment; software manufacturers; and producers of educational television. Philippe worked for Philips CID (Corporate Industrial De-

sign) as Senior Designer, Advanced Projects. He was responsible for (pre)conceptual design, product design, screen graphics and interaction design.

NICK WEST As a new media researcher, West is interested in how interactive technologies can integrate with the surrounding physical community. At New York University's Interactive Telecommunications Program, West produced the "Yorb" interactive TV show, which allowed viewers in Manhattan to enter a "virtual" neighborhood where they could talk and interact with other members of their "real" neighborhood.

No special equipment was required -- just a telephone and a cable TV connection -- so each show received around 5,000 calls. Student designers built interactive spaces within "Yorb" that allowed for dancing, playing music and games among an audience unfamiliar with the conventions of computers or new media.

West's group then created a prototype "Neighborhood Web", an attempt to take the Web out of the computer and put it onto the streets. Using portable computers and Global Positioning Satellite technology, this local version of the World Wide Web will allow the placement of any type of information as a virtual layer on top of our existing built environment.

Currently, West is extending the "Neighborhood Web" concept to include traveling interactive displays that act as "virtual time machines", overlaying views of the historical city on top of the new. As a visiting scholar in Rio de Janeiro, Brazil, he is working in conjunction with the Museu Nacional de Belas Artes and Pontifĺcia Universidade Catolica.

PHILIPPE WEGNER: THE AREA OF MEDIA IS STILL A CHAOS, OR AT LEAST A JUNGLE

DICK RIJKEN: THERE MAY BE A TRADITION IN MEDIA, BUT IT'S MEANINGLESS TO ME RIGHT NOW IN DESIGNING THE KINDS OF MEDIA I'M DESIGNING TODAY

BART LOOTSMA: IN FACT, EVERY DESIGN REWRITES THE HISTORY

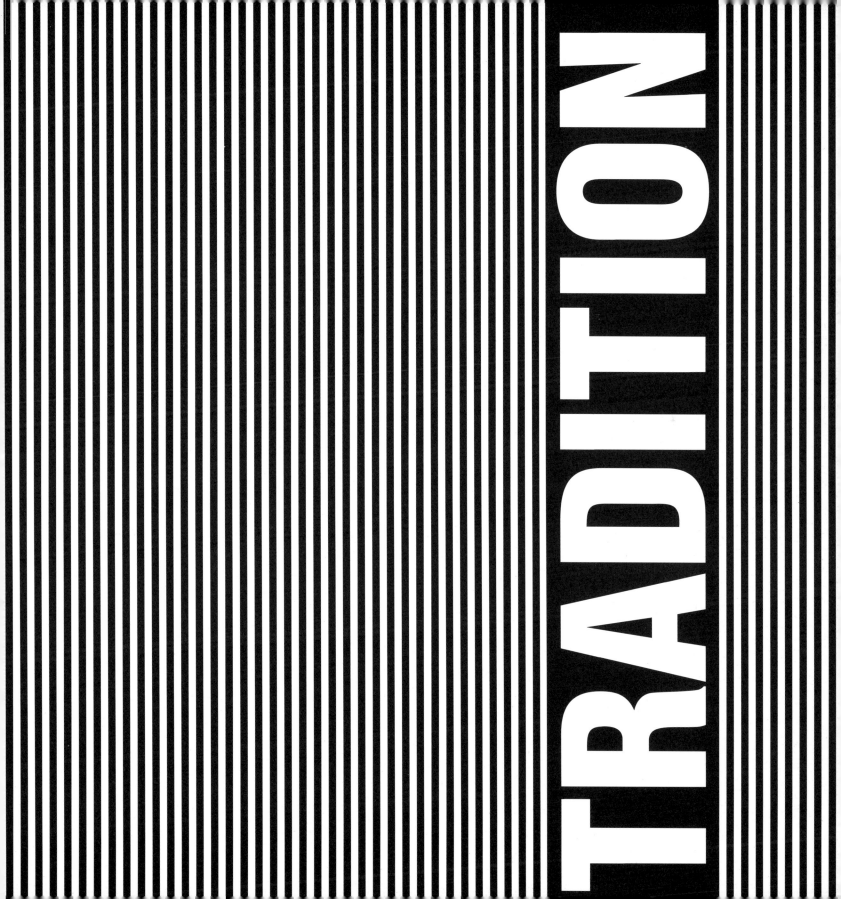

TRADITION

DICK RIJKEN: I see significant differences between media and architecture in regard to tradition. To me, architecture seems a more homogenous field than media. Specifically over the past few decades, the media have become a melting pot of journalism, graphic design, audio-visual media, entertainment, information, computer science, interaction design, various scientific disciplines, etc. Every discipline has its own tradition, and some of them are still very new.

This also causes a lot of misunderstandings amongst media designers. It seems like they're all busy with the same thing, but because they're working from various traditions, they have a completely different image of the issues, activities, objectives and evaluation criteria. This is especially true in the digital media, because within it people from different backgrounds design exactly the same products or processes. I get the impression that it's easier for architecture to map out a clear development over the course of time. To me, as an outsider, this clarity seems to come from the fact that at every stage in architecture's development, there has been a clear set of criteria which could be used to evaluate designs. Alongside the difference in complexity between the traditions of media and architecture, of course there's also the difference in age: the century-old tradition of architecture, compared to the decades (or sometimes only years) of some media. In my opinion, these two differences between the disciplines cause

the discussions in architecture to be clearer, because many ideas have not only been "thought up" before, but they have also almost always actually been tried out at some point in the past. In many discussions during the workshop, the media designers were told that you guys had already tried out this or that once before, but that it amounted to nothing...

BART LOOTSMA: I think it's difficult to judge whether architecture is a more homogeneous field than media. All in all, architecture encompasses about everything, from design to structural product design, urban renewal, urban planning, town and country planning, constructional design and large-scale infrastructural projects. The media world currently seems to be undergoing more development, and that makes it a bit more of a cluttered field. But architecture is also constantly being exposed to social, technological and cultural changes. Thus the decision-making process surrounding architecture, for example, has become more and more complex over the past decades. There are more and more different parties involved in the realization of a design. These continual changes also lead to the fact that the development of architecture over the course of time is not as unambiguous as you suggest. This is easy to see if we look at the map of a random city. We can then fairly clearly distinguish all kinds

PHILIPPE WEGNER: Architecture has an old history, with long-established roots and experiences to learn from. In that sense, the area of media is still a chaos, or at least a jungle. Everybody is making explorations, but there's hardly any experience of the impact of highly interactive media on the public.

WINY MAAS: I think media designers are in a way old-fashioned. You don't have a tradition. You just analyze a lot of things about information, you don't twist it. There's an inherent conflict in this.

GREG LYNN: Architecture is a conservative discipline that constantly tries to transgress itself: it's a way of making itself new. Media started out as a very new discipline; it's a new profession that wants to establish and stabilize itself. So when media looks at architecture they think of architecture in terms of stability, location, place, comfort and friendliness. When architects look at media, they see transgression.

BERT MULDER: It's not so much a question of architecture actually being more traditional, but rather the fact that during the Masterclass, the arguments in architectural professional dialogue tended to be framed within an existing body of reflection. This might just reflect the preference of the people present (architectural theorists versus media pragmatists), or differences between the fields (another kind of reflection in the media field), but the difference in preference was obvious.

WINY MAAS: Architecture is a sort of thinking machine, and it makes structures, delivering facilities to other people. Essentially you just manage a process.

of various fragments which were realized during different periods, during which people had different ideas. Often plans are left incomplete, are thwarted, or are even undone by later plans. This holds true not only for a city like Amsterdam, with a long history, but also for a very new city like Almere. If we also look at the history of architecture in the sense of individual buildings, we often see not only rather sudden changes in typology and style, but over the course of time we also see that there are more and more ideas coexisting side by side. In fact, every design rewrites the history. It's true that there's a long tradition in architecture of absorbing new technical developments. This almost never happens in a uniform way. The histories of architecture, interior design, design and urban planing are closely related. Technical developments have an effect on various levels: first of all directly, as applications, and then via organization, and last but not least on the level of the expression of a worldview and a view of humanity. Almost all technical developments have also left their traces in architecture, and they're still present today. Since architects are aware of this, technical innovation often leads to expanded speculations, which also has consequences for the way architects deal with architecture and media. I think by the way that it's a pity that media designers constantly tend to emphasize only the new aspects of their discipline. Of course there's also a history of the media that goes back much fur-

ther, and which might be able to help today's media designers think about the latest developments. I hope that media designers don't make the same mistake as the industrial designers who believe that design has its origins in industrial production, while this had already been preceded by a phase of manual serial production which was made possible because manual craftsmen learned how to read drawings. By thinking this way, industrial designers not only cut of their ties to history, but this kind of thinking has also led to a lack of broader cultural frame of reference which also contains a specific worldview and a view of humanity. And this remains the case up until today, which stands in the way of a truly creative discussion about the field.

DICK RIJKEN: There are rarely explicit discussions held about worldviews and views of humanity, a fact I regret very much. Which view of humanity underlies a gun? Or a pen? Or an Internet search engine which magically comes up with only Chinese sites, or sites which have been made with Microsoft technology? I think that the distinction between old and new media is relevant here (whereby new is characterized by being digital and interactive). If we're only talking about visual design disciplines like graphic design, then you're completely right: there is a rich history there, and this history is also given appropriate attention in most design education.

NICK WEST: While not discounting the need for historical analysis, the largely undesigned explosion of the World Wide Web has created a new phenomenon. For the first time, millions of examples of media coexist side-by-side in a relatively permanent and publicly viewable installation - an almost architectural installation, in fact, that in many ways resembles a city.

PHILIPPE WEGNER: I don't believe (coming from an industrial design background myself) that industrial designers have such a limited view of their origins. The design of hardware products has always ranged from craftsmanship up to large-scale mass production, along with everything in between. Apart from that, industrial design in Italy, for example, has its basis in architecture even to the extent that the architects are the industrial designers. Do you really believe that because the scale of the "object" changed, they just threw away their views, beliefs and experience?

BERT MULDER: The funny thing with new media is that it's so young, it doesn't have a history. So when we talk, we just babble without being hindered by anything at all. When you talk about the discipline of architecture, every statement forms part of a history of statements. So when you say something is right or wrong, you have to allude to all other arguments. In new media, that's not at all the case.

DICK RIJKEN: There may be a tradition in media, but it's a tradition that's meaningless to me right now in designing the kinds of media I'm designing today.

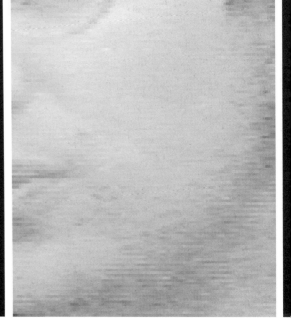

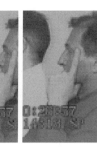

HISTORY OF COMMUNICATION

BART LOOTSMA: Visual design (and what an influence Van Doesburg has had on the jargon, by the way) is only one aspect. I'm referring much more to changes in organization, regarding the organization of the production process, of architecture, of design or of whatever else, as well as regarding the organization of buildings and cities, whereby you can think of infrastructure or typology. I think that you have to incorporate these kinds of aspects in the history of design as well. Think of the influence that various printing techniques have had both on design as well as on the various possibilities which the techniques have offered in the dissemination of the product. If we're talking about the history of the media or of media design, I would never want to exclusively consider the history of graphic design, but rather the history of communication. Then, for example, the infrastructure would once again play a major role, as would the revolutions in that area.

DICK RIJKEN: I completely agree with you there. You can see this very strongly in the media. The broadcast world itself is a very good example of this. Our whole broadcast establishment is rooted in the idea of a scarcity of infrastructure. The production equipment used to be very expensive, and there was a limited number of radio and television channels. So all this had to be handled very carefully. The Netherlands' VPRO broadcaster, for example, is entirely organized on the basis of infrastructure: we have radio, television and a TV guide, with corresponding organizational departments. There used to be three totally separate infrastructures for production, distribution and consumption, and this distinction was meaningful. Now that the equipment is becoming cheaper, the infrastructure is no longer scarce, and all information is becoming digital, this distinction has actually lost its meaning. On my computer I can work with sound, moving images text, you name it... More importantly, I can manipulate these things myself and even distribute them anew. The VPRO's "digital" division has been pleading for years to have another organizational structure for the VPRO, one that's based on categories of content and not on an infrastructural foundation. What we'd most like to see would be editorial and content-based clusters which respond to social issues, whereby a specific media would only be decided upon at a later stage. You can see this in the website (www.vpro.nl), which opens up under the categories of "art/culture", "people/society", "science/technology", "youth" and "humor/amusement". The digital infrastructure makes it simultaneously possible and necessary to work from the basis of content instead of technology.

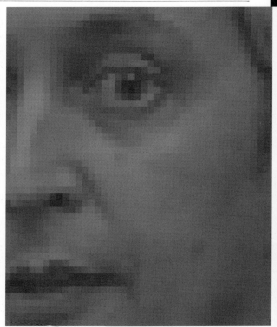

BART LOOTSMA: I think it's important to draw a distinction between the history of design (or architecture) as a history of designers who consciously expressed their ideas in the works themselves (as well as verbally and in writing), and an anonymous history which investigates, for example, the influence of technological innovations on a discipline or phenomenon. In construction, for example, it's not uncommon that technological innovations are first applied by unknown people. Even if a technological innovation has already been used on a large scale, it takes time before architects become aware of it and take advantage of its ultimate possibilities. The closed nature of the disciplinary kind of thinking also often precludes innovations. That's why Le Corbusier got so wound up in "Vers une architecture" about the blind conservatism of his colleagues. An important section of that book, "Des yeux qui ne voient pas", illustrates technical applications which had already been generally accepted in other disciplines such as shipbuilding, airplane construction and the automobile industry, yet which architects had remained oblivious to. Although mostly based on innovations in weaponry, Manuel DeLanda's approach in his book "War in the Age of Intelligent Machines" can serve as an example of a form of historiography based on the consequences of technological innovations. In this book, he shows that these innovations, which often seem very small, also have a delayed reaction on the organizational structure of the army and the means of waging war. It doesn't take a lot of imagination to find analogies with other disciplines, specifically with media design, in this kind of historiography. A kind of second layer of historiography might be able to consider the contribution of designers who deliberately react to, and subsequently give expression to, a given thing.

DICK RIJKEN: At the moment, the new media are very much determined by digital technology. And here we're pretty much talking about a field which has a very short history. The history of information technology can be seen in two ways: from an historical perspective and from a cultural one. From the historical perspective, Henri van Praag, in his book "Verandering" ("Change"), distinguishes five stages in the development of information technology: formal, scientific, technical, social and cultural.
In the seventeenth century, it was discovered that Euclidean geometry (in which everything was based on a 90 degree system) was not the only way of describing reality. A geometry based on 60 degrees was more useable for some phenomena. Thereafter, people were able to prove that there are many possible geometries with an internal consistency which are useable in different contexts. This is a seed of pluralistic thinking: there was no longer a single reality modeled

BERT MULDER: I find the distinction between "anonymous history", design, and designers interesting. Is the creative tension between the anonymous, explicit work of individual designers and the development of a more coherent body of knowledge, such as design, a basic dynamic of innovation? If so, then individuals are a creation as catalysts in two directions: the development of a body of knowledge, as well as new, anonymous development. Innovation becomes the play between the invisible and the visible.

MICHAEL HENSEL: Perhaps poststructural thought once again enabled a broader interdisciplinary mode of communication and collaboration. Today's heuristic, conversational mode of innovation is then not only to be seen as a cultural product, but as the prevailing shaper of cultural production as well. As one of the most immediate examples, one could refer to the conversational mode of this publication, which does not convey the message of the single mastermind, but instead showcases a conversational mediation between multiple identities and thoughts, unfolding heuristic speculations regarding the potential future of interdisciplinary collaboration.

by a theory that would claim to be 'true', but instead there were several models which all yielded something of value in different application contexts, or for different purposes. In the scientific stage (at the beginning of the twentieth century), this thinking was used in the so-called "theory of automata", which theorizes about symbol-processing systems. The best-known example is Alan Turing's Turing machine, an automaton that can emulate any other symbol-processing automaton. In the middle of the twentieth century, this feeds a technical revolution, as we start manufacturing machines that turn these ideas into reality: computers. One piece of hardware runs multiple programs. The Turing Machine still is a dominant explanatory model for computer science scholars. Next (and this stage applies to society in general), computers are brought in for calculations and administrative purposes, and many societal processes become dependent on them. At the same time, the great ideologies begin to lose relevance and we see a strong individualism come to the fore in our society. At the moment, according to Van Praag, we're in the cultural phase. Information technology is very much becoming a culture-determining phenomenon, and computers are no longer only being used for calculations and administration, but for cultural expression and reflection as well. New design disciplines like interaction design arise, that attempt to give a human/cultural face to the technical revolution. The

second way of looking at the history of information technology is from a much narrower defined cultural perspective, in which this recent development of administrative equipment into cultural forms plays a central role. The situation in which we now find ourselves is strongly influenced by the recent history and culture of administration and process control. The English word 'computer' means calculator, as does the German 'Rechner', while the French 'ordinateur' 'arranges'. The computers are not per se rooted in a background which is conducive to cultural expression. Many clients outsource their conceptual designs for digital communication to IT companies or organizational consultants, and the designer is only dug up at a later stage to try and make the whole thing look pretty. There's tragedy in the fact that this is in many cases understandable, primarily because many designers don't think any further than "the image", while the aesthetics of interactivity are much more rooted in action than in visual perception. And that's the reason why the "new" aspect is often emphasized: interaction isn't looking, it's doing. When is there 'beauty' in action? In that sense, the visual tradition doesn't have much to offer us, because it's all about looking. It's the tragedy of the new media: culture is urgently needed, but the appropriate practitioners (designers) too often ask the wrong questions. But there's nothing wrong with using the image as a starting point, as long as action is also

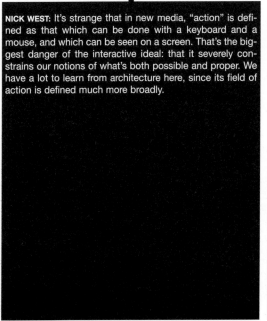

NICK WEST: It's strange that in new media, "action" is defined as that which can be done with a keyboard and a mouse, and which can be seen on a screen. That's the biggest danger of the interactive ideal: that it severely constrains our notions of what's both possible and proper. We have a lot to learn from architecture here, since its field of action is defined much more broadly.

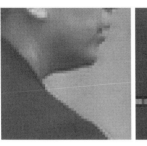

involved in the considerations. The innovations in the field of design are now being thought up more often by creative programmers (with a feel for culture and aesthetics) than by traditional designers.

BART LOOTSMA: My criticism of this kind of historiography is analogous to the one regarding the historiography of design. The use of computers for administrative goals became interesting, for example, because the amount of administrative work has increased explosively over the past century; even before the war, for example at banks, there were already entire armies of pen-pushers keeping money transfers and interest entries up to date in large books, and they were doing so by hand. The cultural aspect doesn't come to the fore only because computers are (suddenly?) being used for individual expression. Something doesn't have a cultural component just because someone who has a degree from an art academy worked on it. The computer and everything that goes along with it form a cultural phenomenon in and of themselves.

DICK RIJKEN: This very much has to do with a broader definition of "culture". I recently heard someone referring to an XTC pill as a "helper application" (a term from the world of Internet browsers) ...

COLLABORATION

DICK RIJKEN: In regard to the collaboration amongst media designers, I often use the model of the rock band. Many bands are true collectives: there's no single person who's the auteur, but instead all the musicians work together on a final result. You can see them even now, the first multimedia bands: someone for the visuals, someone for sound, someone for software, with all the ideas being developed together, and the various tasks only being assigned at a later stage. There's no single individual who claims the cultural dimension. The US is doing better in this regard than the Netherlands. Here, there's still an attitude amongst designers of, "I think it up, and the programmer carries out my ideas", while often it's precisely in the programming that the key to the aesthetics of the interactivity lies.

The difference in backgrounds between the designer and the programmer is also echoed in the way the developed products are considered. In rough terms, media designers tell "stories", while computer scientists make "tools". Now we're seeing websites which contain "stories" as well as "tools", sometimes even totally integrated. But the thinking regarding the tools has long been utilitarian, while the making of stories and pictures has to do with ethics and aes-

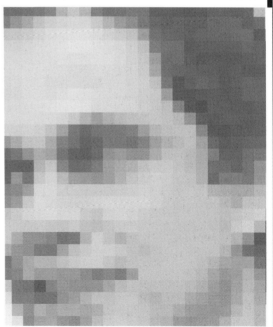

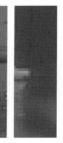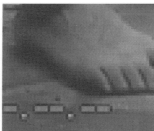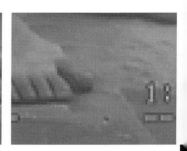

thetics. Thus you see two traditions meeting one another in the new media: design disciplines affiliated with art, and engineering disciplines affiliated with technical science. They're totally different cultures with different habits, views of humanity, worldviews and value systems.

BART LOOTSMA: Don't get me wrong, but on a number of points I get a feeling of deja vu, and I don't think what you're talking about here specifically has to do with the digital revolution. In the history of architecture, after all, we see way back at the beginning of the previous century the split between the Ecole Polytechnique and the Ecole des Beaux Arts, both of whom approached architecture in different ways: one in a constructional way, the other in an architectural way, which of course led to different architectures arising within both schools. The grounds for this schism were in technological innovations, and even until today it's still possible to trace various architectural ideas and schools (the curriculum) back to this. Here is an eternal discussion regarding the shortcomings and advantages of one compared to the other. Collaborations between various disciplines have already long been institutionalized in architecture, since the architect has to work together with many various parties in order to get a project realized: the client, the city, builders, equipment experts, suppliers and contractors. But on a purely design level as well, there were already quite a few firms back in the sixties who used the example of the rock band, from Ricardo Bofill's Taller de Architectura in Spain, England's Archigram, the Austrian groups like Hans Rucker Co. and Coop Himmelblau, all the way to the Italian Superstudio and Archizoom. But on the more everyday level of the commercial "corporate office" as well, there's the cliché of "the office that has everything in-house." So whether we're talking about the specific model of the rock band or other kinds of collaborations, I think that interdisciplinary collaboration is a much broader social phenomenon, which in many areas arises out of necessity. According to British sociologist Anthony Giddens, it's a phenomenon which is connected to the "second modernity", in which authority does not necessarily have to do (or at least not to a great extent) with a general, perhaps God-given wisdom, as it does in the traditional society, but has to do instead with specialized expertise. Since the specialized expertise is decentralized per definition, we live in a world of "multiple authorities." And every one of these "multiple authorities" is only an expert within his own field, within which he is subjected to legislation by a branch organization or by jurisprudence. As soon as he steps outside of this field, he immediately becomes a layman like anyone else. Collaboration on the basis of equality is thus inevitable, and we see this not only with architects, film

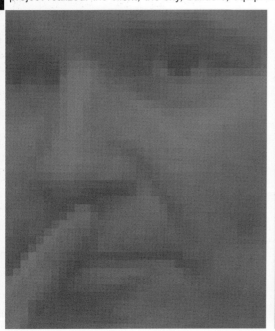

MICHAEL HENSEL: Architecture is not only design. Part of the process is organizational negotiation between what is possible and what is desirable, particularly in terms of urban design. It's becoming increasingly clear that you have so many groups of interest, you can't just make a master plan and deliver it as a product. Architects have to guide processes for long time spans; therefore it seems highly interactive.

MICHAEL HENSEL: In the discipline of architecture, the associative reference to the rock band hardly seems to work. Most of the given examples do truly work as "vertical" corporate structures (although that might also be true of today's rock bands and their managerial structures). There are some more recent examples though, such as the OCEAN network, in which a horizontal and truly decentralized and decorporized network structure guides the mode of operativity and productivity. Here, one may argue, Deleuze's radically horizontal school of thought finds its collaborative manifestation.

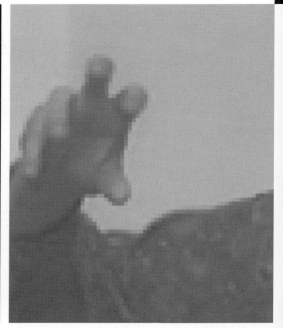

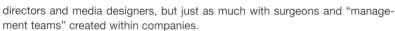

directors and media designers, but just as much with surgeons and "management teams" created within companies.

DICK RIJKEN: The argument can indeed be extended to all kinds of collaborations between various disciplines. The fact is that the information society in particular is characterized by complex networks of relations, in which there is more collaboration than ever before.

BART LOOTSMA: I think that digitalization makes the collaboration between various disciplines a lot easier because the same data can be processed in various ways by different members of a team: an architect's digitized drawings can also be used, for example, by the building engineer, the constructor and the contractor, and it becomes easier to give feedback on their information during the design process.

DICK RIJKEN: Exactly! I think we can hardly oversee the consequences of a common infrastructure.

MICHAEL HENSEL: Today, interdisciplinary collaboration can go beyond the linear development of digital datasets towards manufacturing, as in passing digital files from architect to engineer to manufacturer. In the OCEAN network, for example, furniture, urban design, architecture and graphic design can be informed and generated by a shared initial dataset. The linear development of digital files towards production processes then becomes an integral part of multiplicitous cross-disciplinary applications of shared datasets. These shared datasets enable cross-disciplinary collaboration, serve as a common design tool, and allow for coherent reflection upon the various resultant products, thereby delivering a shared generic infrastructure aiming at multiplicituous production.

PHILIPPE WEGNER: MEDIA TRY TO CREATE ORDER IN A WORLD OF CHAOS

WINY MAAS: MEDIA DESIGNERS ARE MOSTLY INTERESTED IN ORGANIZING. ARCHITECTS ARE INTERESTED IN DISORGANIZING

BART LOOTSMA: MEDIA DESIGNERS SHOULD BE MORE CONSCIOUS OF THE SIDE EFFECTS OF TREIR PROPOSALS

BERT MULDER: HOW A HOUSE BECOMES A "HOME" IS CONSIDERED BY ARCHITECTS TO BE AN OLD-FASHIONED WOOLLY SOCKS ISSUE

DICK RIJKEN: "TOO BAD, BETTER LUCK NEXT TIME"

LARS SPUYBROEK: ONE IS OFTEN BETTER A SLAVE FOR THE WRONG REASONS THAN THE IMAGINARY MASTER OVER FUNCTIONAL BONDAGE

USER VS. DESIGNER

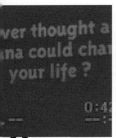

BART LOOTSMA: Media designers have the tendency to place "the person" and "the individual" centrally, without conceptualizing these issues. Thus, "the person" and "the individual" run the risk of being cuddled to death by good intentions. Furthermore, individuals are detached from their social contexts. A good example is the recent discussion in the Netherlands regarding the ethics of the Albert Heijn supermarket's Bonus Card. You're offered a card which can spare you a lot of money - great, right? - yet which on the other hand mercilessly registers your purchasing behavior without you having any idea of what happens with this data. I think that media designers should have to be more conscious of the side effects of their proposals.

Architects, even in the case of individual villas, never work exclusively for "the individual" or for the client. They always have to responsibly take society into account. This might have to do with the way their designs will interfere with others (for example by taking away sun or disturbing the view), or the way they change the look of the environment, the way they encumber the city's infrastructure (consider the meter cabinet), or even in their use of materials which might, for example, need to be both fireproof and environmentally friendly at the same time. There have even been government institutions created to supervise all these sorts of things.

ETHICS

DICK RIJKEN: Proposals for something like the Bonus Card aren't made by the designers, but by employees from the marketing and sales departments. What happens here is a typical example of the fact that in designing services, a designer is only called in when the actual Bonus Card (and then only the actual card itself) needs to be given a form. The question with the Bonus Card is whether we're really talking about design; do "service design" and "business design" really fall under the category of design? But it's clear that the debate regarding privacy is grounded in the considerations on the media.

BART LOOTSMA: But Dick, what about your teamwork and your rock band? You can't distance yourself from the other members of the team just like that as soon as there's criticism, can you?

DICK RIJKEN: My whole point here is that these people are not in the same band, they're not playing together. We can launch a whole big issue here and cry out that our privacy is being jeopardized, but the discussion only becomes interesting if we think beyond that. The bigger context is an increasing degree of open-

PHILIPPE WEGNER: The way it's described here, the responsibility mainly targets measurable things. That kind of focus of responsibility can be found in industrial design and media design as well. But what about emotions such as feelings of safety, comfort, likes, dislikes, etc.? To what extend is the image of the user taken seriously, by architects as well? Are our new suburbs the jewel in the crown?

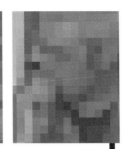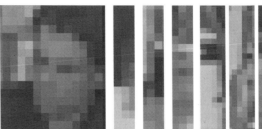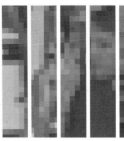

ness everywhere in our society. Even companies are being exposed to this. Heineken wanted to invest in Burma, but the public didn't think that was a good idea and the whole deal fell through. Shell was messing about in Nigeria and they knew it. New ways will (have to) be found (by all involved parties) to deal with this openness. Since consumers have an ever greater need to have a say in how companies handle ethical issues, we'll be seeing some interesting constructs in the near future. Privacy might become a product: "don't violate privacy, sell it." Ethics as the basis for commerce?

BART LOOTSMA: I don't know if all of this has to do with openness. And furthermore, there is indeed a difference between privacy and a company's openness, certainly in the case of a multinational which can avoid traditional national legislation. But in practice, this openness has to be forced, and this only happens when things go wrong on a grand scale. The question is whether the steadily increasing power of the consumer will be able to force this. Can this power be an alternative to traditional national legislation? And what role will designers play in facilitating these changes? I don't think that in the future we'll be able to look at multinational companies as sorts of futuristic political parties which we'll vote for by either buying or not buying their products. The difference between a multi-

national and a political party, after all, is the multinational's self-interest, which is expressed in its striving for profit maximization. A political party, first and foremost, always has to keep the general welfare in mind. Whether the power of the consumer offers a safe alternative to the cross-border behavior of multinationals remains to be seen. But for this to be the case, journalism and (international) interest groups like environmental and human rights organizations first have to undergo a considerable evolution. The image that your comments conjure up is one of an international capitalism in its most terrifying form. I think that designers play a role in these changes in that they continuously have to think about the consequences of their actions. In so doing, they can take an example from architects, who have always discussed the social consequences of their designs and derived codes of behavior as a result. That's why we also have arrangements amongst doctors, lawyers, notaries and so forth, right? Regardless of that, the discourse, however abstract it may seem, plays an important role in the arrangements that architects have with one another. The architect is by definition held accountable by society, and has been for a long time. Architecture is (not only) a consumer article.

How do media designers consider these kinds of ethical issues? It often strikes me that media designers actually see themselves as kinds of squatters, using

GREG LYNN: There's a funny symmetry from the 70s to the 90s: it used to be ad men in leisure suits talking about the emergence of advertising through print, television, radio and events. It seems troubling that what Dick is talking about could be placed along that trajectory. Interactivity has always been the term on which social and economic theories of consumption are based.

BERT MULDER: Both authors make similar remarks on the role of professionals and the consequences of their work in a larger context. The growing possibilities of IT make new and more complex systems possible, and that may be the reason why the larger consequences of these things are just now entering into the equation. Hence the thin quality of their design. In design education, people are now starting to recognize the need for the awareness of a bigger picture, in general design as well as in media design. Both need to address the consequences of their actions in social, economic or ecological terms. This is a remark on a more open attitude required of professional media designers in a multi-disciplinary field, and I couldn't agree more. The same holds true for architects for whom the distinction between architecture and urban planning becomes blurred, and you simultaneously act within both. There is no escape, and every architecture is a statement in urban planning.

the technology of big business for the ordinary person; thus they don't feel that they have to ask themselves these kinds of questions. The myths of Apple vs. Microsoft and Netscape vs. Explorer play an important role in maintaining this heroic image, as does the myth of the Internet being a subversive use of a network that was actually developed for defense purposes.

DICK RIJKEN: It's interesting that you mention doctors, lawyers and notaries. Where do their codes of behavior come from? Government? Or from a complex interaction between the market, practioners, and legislators? With regard to media design, I think we're dealing here with the many-times-nothing effect. No great steps which have very major consequences are taken all at once. It's noteworthy that the Bonus Card caused so much discussion, while people have been saving Air Miles for years, a system which actually couples a lot more data together. These sorts of developments come gradually, and that's why it's so difficult for designers to keep an eye on when a particular border is being crossed. Furthermore, there's the question of whether designers themselves have a clear notion of what or where the borders are...
Another important phenomenon here is the knowledge that communicating parties have about one another. This applies to commerce as well: on the basis of

their knowledge of clients, companies can allow their products or services to better fit their public. Specifically in the field of information, the fact is that personal, knowledge-driven communication is becoming an increasingly important requirement in dealing with the information overload. Trust is a central issue in these relationships. If I don't take you into confidence, then you can't help me in the way that I want to be helped. And you don't make any money... You will have to earn my trust.

EVOLUTION

DICK RIJKEN: I very much get the impression that the way an architectural design plays a role within the architectural discourse (which develops from the tradition) is a crucial element in evaluating the quality of a design. This plays a much smaller role in media design. This does exist, but criteria which have their origins in the application context seem much more important. "Does it communicate?" is often the most important question.
I also get the impression that architects have a lot of difficulty dealing with the utility context in evaluating the quality of a design: how well does the design fit into the situation it ends up in? A reason for this might be that architects simply

GREG LYNN: Architects stopped claiming 40 years ago that design was an instrument of cultural and social change on a global scale, as they imply a behind-the-scenes totalitarian regime. Perhaps digital media assume that this kind of political and economic armature is not related to new technologies, but Microsoft seems to make a strong counter-argument to that assumption. Again, architecture and media design are probably more similar than either discipline might like to admit.

WINY MAAS: Furthermore, media designers are more obsessed by the individual than they are with massiveness. Urbanism, on the other hand, has an historical relation to massiveness and massive events. Architects need to preplan for hypothetical or assumed individuals, so they never really deal with individuals. Media designers also deal with assumed viewers, but they will have feedback within a year or less. We have to wait six or seven years before we hear a reaction.

BERT MULDER: It's noteworthy that the notion of "the person" doesn't actually come up in architecture. The person is indeed present as an abstract thing, for example as a pattern of movement in a house or as a stream of people through a street, but never as a person who experiences things. In the designing of cities and buildings, the efficiency and form of things is the most important consideration. It's simply that the Western way of thinking is very much geared towards form and towards making things. We don't care how it's made, or how we remember it, or how it ultimately falls apart. This also applies to architecture: a house is a thing, and it has to have a living room and a bedroom.

But the questions of how a person experiences a house and how a house becomes a "home" are considered by architects to be old-fashioned, open sandals and woolly socks issues. This is especially significant in the media, since the audience for whom a program is made is a major consideration there. If media designers and architects collaborate, it might well be that the experience of the person will return to architecture.

BRUNO FELIX: The amount of information on offer is becoming greater and more complex, the information itself is becoming faster and more individualized, and the production of information is becoming cheaper and cheaper. Since designers are therefore beginning to operate within a growing supply of information, with more and more possibilities, they have to cut to the essence of the people they want to reach. Thus they have to consistently place users centrally in their designs in order to keep serving them and to ensure that their ideas can be used and be found. This design mentality is becoming increasingly important in media and information, and I think that architects can learn something from this.

produce less than media designers do: every week another poster, every week a new TV show, every month another website, or a new interface for an existing website, every six months a new campaign. This might also explain why media designers generally operate within a less intellectual discourse than architects; architects simply have more time to reflect upon their projects. If a media designer doesn't succeed in achieving an objective, it's often "too bad, better luck next time." This also allows a kind of reflection within the actual actions themselves, while verbal reflection becomes less important. Another notion is 'evolution'. Specifically the new media are characterized by evolution, rather than by design. I get the impression that the evolution of buildings is becoming a notion that architects are just starting to take into account in their work. How long will a building last? What will happen to it over time? How can fast-evolving information environments resonate with slow structures like buildings? Questions like these... And I also get the impression that amongst many architects, the utility context is such a loaded term because quite a few architects have had their fingers burned by translating specific ideals into specific buildings which were then supposed to bring about specific behavior. That's why it seems that a kind of escape has come about in form.

GREG LYNN: To say that media design happens quickly and architectural design happens slowly is frankly ridiculous, as the volume and speed of the design and construction of cities, buildings and interiors around the world far exceeds the design of "posters, TV shows and websites". Although cities are more material, such a statement proves to be absolutely ridiculous when critically tested. What is most interesting, though, is not the falsity of such statements, but rather their motivation. It might be that the opposition between architecture and media design in these pages reflects the fact that it's difficult to define what digital media is without defining it as NOT ARCHITECTURE. I would propose that if media design is going to develop a coherent discourse about itself, it should stop defining itself against architecture as this simplifies and falsifies both sets of activities.

NICK WEST: A house is a definite product of an architectural process, while in the media there is often no endpoint. A chat room is not a result; the product of a chat room is an ongoing process of people conversing. This seems different from a living room, which can contain a conversation, but the architect gets the final say because the room is architecturally defined before the people move in.

PHILIPPE WEGNER: The difference in the speed of the design (media design fast, architectural design slow) and the resulting differences in process (trial and error, complete new design versus evolutionary design or living for a long time with the consequences of the result) and attitude are, in my view, not an accurate representation of what's happening in the "media design projects" dealing with core processes within, for example, companies. Especially in projects where the stand-alone product loses ground in both technological infrastructure as well as in communication infrastructure, development processes tend to take more and more throughput time instead of ensuring shorter time-spans due to issues such as underlying systems becoming larger, and tying together systems which previously had no link whatsoever. I myself am involved in task-supporting systems in the banking environment, which were started in 1993 and which are still under development. The same is true for the growing number of websites which contain much more than simple digitized information pages. You don't just throw these systems away every year but instead elaborate upon them further. The way that the use of these media is slowly becoming a little more mature already reflects this change.

GREG LYNN: Look at housing done in the United States: the developers do these cookie card blocks, which everybody wants. They want homogeneity, they want a certain degree of flexibility, but they don't want interactive design. This is what architecture found out a long time ago. Look at the percentage of housing designed in the United States by architects. It is less than 1%, while in the 60s it used to be more than 10%. Not only are people not interested in houses designed by architects, but they're not interested in interactivity, either. They just want to buy something off the shelf.

PHILIPPE WEGNER: The user is not very interested in creating, modifying or elaborating upon what he or she has been given as a toolkit. Maybe I'm not so interested in sitting around with architects to decide what kind of house would be perfect for me. But once I have it, all of a sudden some

BART LOOTSMA: The answer to this question flows from my answer to the last one. If we're purely talking about the use of a design, then architects confer with their client, who is then partially responsible for the design's usability. In complicated assignments, the help of specialized consultancy firms is called in. But seeing to it that the design is useful for the client is only part of the architect's task. In fact, the architect's profession is quite a strange one: he's paid by a client who wants value for his money, but he also has to ensure that the way the client manifests himself outwardly and the way the design will appear in public are in accordance with what society considers acceptable. In a strict sense, you could even say that this is the only aspect of the architect's work which is truly "architectural." As we all know, the form that buildings assume within the city plays an important role for the general public, and thus it's not unusual for a good deal of the architectural debate to revolve around this concern. Of course this can degenerate into a kind of escape, but it seems to me that it's an over-simplification to suggest that this applies to architecture as a whole.

I also have the feeling that some media designers are much more involved with form than architects are, and that there's hardly any imaginable field in which the desire for user-friendliness is so much ignored. Most of the products I see hardly get beyond the gimmick level, and in purely functional terms they have little

things are wrong. Then I want the house to be flexible enough so that it can change to my changing needs. Is the VPRO building designed to accommodate the way the VPRO works today, or to anticipate a new way of functioning of the VPRO as well?

WINY MAAS: What is interesting is how to work with uncertainty. This happens a lot in building construction: you don't know what will happen ten years from now. You use a certain hypothesis in designing. This hypothesis can only be discussed with a small group of people. It's hard to say if it's really VPRO or not. In that way it's an experiment.

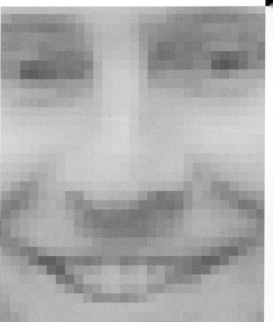

more to offer than a thin first layer: the homepage looks nice, but then there's rarely much more. Many things simply work badly or slowly, there aren't any instructions available (or if there are, they immediately assume the dimensions of a telephone book), and help-desks are arrogant, rude, or simply unreachable. It's really not a pretty picture. If a media designer doesn't succeed in his aim, as you write, it's often a case of "too bad, better luck next time." An architect would never be able to allow himself this kind of attitude, but I don't think a media designer can either. Who's actually responsible in a case like this? Can the client ask for his money back?

Even worse, I find that media designers often have the tendency to pass off their failures onto users' and clients' lack of knowledge. It's like a computer game. You're placed in a labyrinth and have to go looking for the grail, while along the way you have to knock out or sidestep all kinds of monsters and obstacles. Nice as a pastime, but with a moral which stems from the Middle Ages.

DICK RIJKEN: I hope it's clear from my other remarks that I also detest both "gimmick thinking" as well as an avoidance of responsibility to the user and client. By "too bad, better luck next time", my goal is to foster an embracing of responsibility by means of placing change and feedback as central concepts in the design process. Everything is dynamic. Digital media give form to processes (one form of dynamics) and these processes themselves are also subject to change (a second form of dynamics). I'll explain both. First of all, the dynamic product: digital media facilitate users' actions within situations. The situations and the processes are often complex, and are largely unpredictable. Just as with designed spaces, I think that designs are sometimes used in ways which never could have been foreseen, or perhaps flaws come to light which never could have been predicted. The advantage of digital media is that designs can be revised. This revision isn't a way of avoiding responsibility. It's taking the unpredictability of an ever more complex world seriously: looking openly at the way a design will be used in practice, and being prepared to (drastically) revise a design if it doesn't work. Secondly, regarding the dynamic context: functionality sometimes breeds desire for more functionality. Only since the VPRO began its cinema service (which keeps users informed about films on television) have users developed a need for something similar for movie theaters. Or video rental stores. Or film festivals. Sometimes you can't imagine the demand and the actual use beforehand, sometimes you just want to offer the foundation as soon as possible in order to grow later, and sometimes it's even a case of dosage and timing, of introducing small steps within a much larger process (and in the case

BERT MULDER: I must say I agree with the remark on the poor quality of media design and I agree that it's "not a pretty picture". Like in architecture, we're drowning in bland design, sloppy execution, and rows of products that are expressly designed as endless variations on the minimum legal surface area. Of course there are differences in the sloppiness: in the material world, when a minimal structural coherence is largely achieved, a basic functional coherence is usually there in the immaterial world as well. But beyond that... Luckily mediocrity is not inspiration, but rather raw material showing us what to avoid.

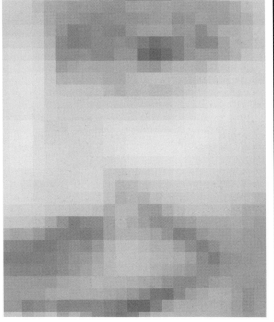

LARS SPUYBROEK: "User" is a utilitarian notion. That means that behavior gets its profile from the machine it uses - the first product of a machine is its "user". We should be very sensitive and careful with words like use and action, in addition to behavior, habituation, reflexes, misuse, experiment and play. If a machine were only a thing that guides and smoothens human behavior, it would just be another way of replacing human action (as Bill Gates and Bernard Hulsman would like to have it: technology as the perfect butler). Machines are more often levers and accelerators of behavior, and instead of satisfying the "needs of users", they very often destabilize and charge action into something outside of the programmed. Their unconscious is far larger than any manual.

of software producers, clearly with a commercial intent). Evolutionary design with an eye for the reality of situations means that it doesn't have to be complete and perfect all at once.

THE IMAGE OF THE USER

BART LOOTSMA: "The new media can further humanity, but we have to guard against fetishism," says Alain Finkielkraut (De Groene Amsterdammer, February 11, 1998). "Technology has freed us from the magic, but along the way technology has become our new magic. The conviction that the Web will result in a pacification of human relationships is a relapse to the most absurd kind of fetishism. Yet to me it seems more ridiculous than dangerous. What I do consider dangerous is the coming about of an elite who show an unbelievable contempt for all those who don't have access to the new media. The gap between the two is large. Furthermore, the elite are not inclined to seal this gap, but instead would rather enlarge it. Those who are familiar with the new media live in an elitist, cosmopolitan world. Those who know nothing about it remain, as ever, bound to where they live.

The Web's elite situate themselves in the leftist corner, and consider everyone else to be reactionary. The fact that entire social groups are left to fend for themselves is dangerous." By your tendency of constantly emphasizing the new and unique aspects of the media, by focusing on a one-sided relationship with the user, by handling architecture a priori as a reactionary and backward field, and above all by the "too bad, better luck next time" attitude, I increasingly get the tendency to endorse the above view.

DICK RIJKEN: Granted, fetishism can be dangerous. But the discussion is not about access. In the early stages, the technologies are expensive, but in this case that's only temporary. A Sony Playstation costs less than a video recorder or a television. Almost everyone has a telephone and can make calls without worrying about the phone bill. The newsagent on the corner sells an endless amount of cheap magazines. There are more computers on the factory floor of an automotive shop than there are in the office of a top manager. There are already scores of cable broadcasters penetrating every living room. Access won't be the problem, if even only because industry benefits from wide-scale accessibility. But what do we talk about during these telephone calls? Which magazine should I buy? Why?

BART LOOTSMA: Do you realize that we're talking about amounts here which are

NICK WEST: Half the people in the world have never made a telephone call. Is this somehow a moral argument against creating intelligently-designed telephone services?
Moreover, the new media form a wildly democratizing force. The cost of putting up a web page - with automatic international distribution via the Internet - is many times smaller than the cost of publishing a magazine or book or TV show with the same international distribution.

LARS SPUYBROEK: Fetishism is quite an intelligent approach towards the object, certainly the technological object. One is often better a slave for the wrong reasons than the imaginary master over functional bondage. Fetishism, hypes, and gadgets are all beyond designer control, and all of them occur like social catastrophes because here, desire for the technological exceeds the need for service.

still high not only for Dutch people, but which would cost a whole year's salary for a large part of the world's population?

DICK RIJKEN: Of course, you have to place my statements within the context of our Western culture (as we also do for your statements up until now, by the way). And here we've now come so far that many people today have a better PC at home than they do at their workplace, and the costs of using the infrastructure are plummeting. And, by the way, how many people (even in the Western world) can afford high-quality architecture?

BART LOOTSMA: Until recently there were quite a few. The building of public housing complexes was, at least in Europe, a guarantee of a high average standard in regard to architecture. Now it's up to the market, and we're seeing districts which are spreading like mold and squandering the landscape, while the standard of the individual flats they consist of is scandalously bad, both constructionally and architecturally, because people find it so important that their houses look personal and different. This is not least of all the result of the emphasis that the public media places on outward appearances. I don't believe that this is being considered very carefully.

DICK RIJKEN: The potential dangers of information technology exist in the realm of apathy: no longer being able to comprehend, no longer being able to keep up (despite accessibility), no longer wanting to keep up, and ending up giving up. The dangers exist in the network society's tendency of simply becoming too complex, too unpredictable, too fast. The only way to survive in a world without certainties, a world which constantly demands choices, is by knowing what you want. And that's not something that happens automatically. How can we deal with complexity? I find that designers have a moral responsibility to involve themselves in the problems. I also don't understand remarks like "it is the role of the VPRO to destabilize its audience", as someone clamored during the Masterclass. You have to be very careful with remarks like these because they touch upon the moral core of the discussion. The current situation is already experienced by many people as chaotic, and that won't get better all by itself. The sometimes rather 'touchy-feely' inclination towards order and harmony that you come across amongst new media designers often stems from an honest social and personal involvement. Strategies for dealing with complexity are geared towards techniques of seeing the essences behind the ostensible chaos, or towards making use of intuition, when rational reflection has become impossible. Do we then have to expect all citizens to be able to effortlessly juggle complex thought processes, or develop new intuitive powers overnight?

BERT MULDER: I'm still wondering about the statement on public housing and the "high average standard", and I also think examples of public initiatives and poor quality can be found. This holds equally true for the market. But if both public and market structures may cause excellence or poor quality, what are the real qualities distinguishing good from bad? What checks and balances do we need to introduce, achieve, and maintain a basic measure of quality in either approach? In media, this is a vital question because these new infrastructures that will become basic to society are just now being built up.

WINY MAAS: The big difference between the two worlds of media and architecture is that media designers are mostly interested in order and organizing, whereas architects are interested in disorganizing or stopping organizing.

PHILIPPE WEGNER: In the Masterclass I noticed how architecture works from a world of order seeking chaos, as there is already too much order. Media try to create order in a world of chaos. One discipline tries to deconstruct order, the other tries to integrate the world. These are notions that you are aware of unconsciously, but that are made much more explicit working with architects. And that reflexivity offers a new perspective on my own discipline.

BART LOOTSMA: Talk about cynicism... I think that we have different definitions of it. I think that people are much more intellectually capable than you believe. That some media designers' penchant for harmony and order is stiff doesn't upset me too much in and of itself. As long as there are also moments in which the complexity or the problems which are glossed over by the stiffness are brought to light, in which the tranquilized and patronized audience is forced to wake up, for example by being thrown just a little bit off kilter. This has long been the VPRO's raison d'être. If I were a designer, I would personally consider it a challenge to make a design which leaves the complexity of the world intact and which actually challenges users to adopt a more complex picture of the world themselves. This is an attitude which is coming to the fore amongst many architects I respect, and one which I also foster when I discuss a building or design as a critic. I believe that this can work, and that it does work, and that it makes people wiser, more independent and more mature. That's my form of idealism.

DICK RIJKEN: You're acting as if harmony and order are at odds with leaving complexity intact. It is expressly this complexity that you should make understandable to as many people as possible. Clarity is a good means of waking people up. Is your idealism structurally any different than mine, or is it just a question of phrasing?

BART LOOTSMA: I think that, considered from a psychological and philosophical standpoint, it's also much more important to teach people how to deal with misfortune and complexity.

DICK RIJKEN: First of all, the Web's elite don't at all situate themselves in a leftist corner. I don't know of any specific research into the political profiles of "the Web elite", but I see just as many people with a pronounced right-liberal signature (WIRED) as I do with a leftist one. But what's perhaps more interesting is that almost no one wastes words in terms of declaring his or her position in the traditional "left vs. right" political spectrum. Politics is rarely a dimension. That's not to say that many ideas and systems don't (potentially) have political implications, but rather that they aren't actively formulated from that perspective. The question is whether we should be happy with that. I still think it's a good idea to emphasize the new aspects of the new media. Better that than discovering later that we've underestimated the changes, and that we have to react headlong to painful surprises. In regard to the relationship to the user, I have a few things to say. First of all, the user is a part of the situation. Without him or her, there's no interaction.
If you have nothing to do with a particular website, then you're not going to

LARS SPUYBROEK: Apathy is a true philosophical attitude, maybe even more so than fetishism is. Better still than the old nineteenth century ennui. Consumers' melancholy - NOT knowing what you want (but knowing your desires) - resists the idea of "expressing your needs".

PHILIPPE WEGNER: Yes, but I think the border is not so much defined by the intellectual capabilities as it is by the speed of change and the overload of required information. To keep my computer a valuable, up-to-date tool, I have to invest a lot of time. Problems of programs or extensions not working together in harmony... It's like the old automobile, you have to know what happens under the hood. And with the pace at which things change, I doubt we'll reach the kind of stability we have with today's cars. I wonder how we can incorporate space for reflection within media design, space for exchange of experiences, etc., to the scale that a vast majority of designers can perform on a quality level. Or is reality in architecture not so much different (and I mean beyond issues such as safety, construction, etc.)?

BRUNO FELIX: Observing the complexity of the world, leaving it intact and then reflecting it back should, if all is well, be only one of the many things a designer or media maker wants to do. A second is that he also wants to provide insight into this complexity so that a user is given the opportunity to situate himself in regard to what is happening around him. To achieve this, a good way of interesting people in a particular subject can be to surprise him by introducing an unknown perspective, example or argument into a discussion. Yet this is merely a device of the media. The real goal is to provide insight into the complexity. The latter is easier to achieve with media than it is with architecture, namely by not only showing what's happening in the world, but also by reflecting upon it, by weighing arguments, and by introducing different perspectives within a single media manifestation. Behind this difference in possibilities, perhaps there is a difference between the architect and the media designer lurking as well.

BERT MULDER: In a time where we have exponentially rising complexity, we create these generic subset systems in order to control the complexity, and then we create layers to

control them, and then layers to control the layers. We didn't create a product today, or over the past few days, we didn't even design anything. We tried to create a new design methodology. Before that, we were creating a new language, and so we were going in the direction of ethics and morals. We need to create fields, not objects, we need to create processes rather than products and services; we need to create values. This story is not based on idealism. With more people on the planet, we have rising complexity on the outside, extensively, and on the inside, intensively. And both need to be managed or else the complexity will be uncontrollable. We work on a new design methodology not because we want it, but because we need it. Because we need to survive.

LARS SPUYBROEK: It's the same old engineering and enlightenment mistake to think that when you supply the world with structures that shape clarity, light and transparency, you're shaping the basis for freedom of action. I would actually try to argue the opposite, and would hesitate to wake anybody up (and have them keep on wandering in the dark or sleepwalking).

come into contact with any of its content. I get the impression that in dealing with the immediate user, there are major differences between the designing of new media and architecture. Secondly, where are the borders of the designer's activities or responsibilities? Something like strategically embedding a communications product within a business vision is rarely developed by designers, but rather by specialized strategists or other communications professionals. They look at the users from other perspectives, ranging from market research in combination with strategic analysis to an analysis of users' "clicking behavior" or the number of 'hits' that a web page gets. Often an actual design is prefaced by defining a system of target groups, each with their own basic assumptions regarding communications.

BART LOOTSMA: But come on, Dick, this is a pretty formal and defensive position. It's the safeguarding of the old-fashioned professional who doesn't look beyond the borders of his work, even if the attitude of "you ask, we do it" is very refined. But I really thought you were after something else when you were going on about a multidisciplinary approach! Why not a more open attitude? I can't imagine that you guys entered into this experiment only to convert architecture to your new faith?

DICK RIJKEN: It's not about safeguarding. It's about the borders of the designer's field. I'm a firm advocate of defining the designer's field of activity as broadly as possible. I strongly believe that the cultural dimension doesn't stop with the form. It's an attitude which causes a lot of differences of opinion within the design world. Many people consider the image as the central item in a design. Sometimes the distinction is made between "stylists" and "designers", where the "stylist" is geared towards form, while the designer has a much broader view and plays more the role of a "problem solver." Perhaps we should be talking about "designing" instead of "the designer" so that we can thoroughly involve the greater context in the discussion.

I very much get the impression that there's a very clear debate in architecture revolving around form, a debate which is of a very aesthetic character. In the new media, there are a lot of debates taking place at the moment being fed by many other disciplines, debates which are rooted in pluralistic thinking. In short: you guys have just one conversation, while we prefer to simultaneously apply a number of perspectives to a given problem, and then even go so far as to let the various perspectives formally discount one another. How much openness do you want? We want to learn, not only about architecture, but about other disciplines as well.

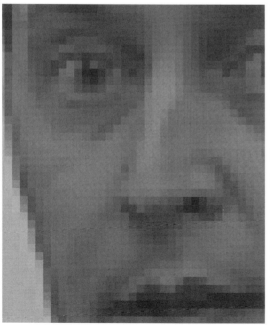

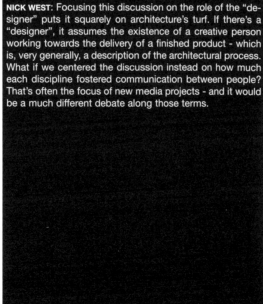

NICK WEST: Focusing this discussion on the role of the "designer" puts it squarely on architecture's turf. If there's a "designer", it assumes the existence of a creative person working towards the delivery of a finished product - which is, very generally, a description of the architectural process. What if we centered the discussion instead on how much each discipline fostered communication between people? That's often the focus of new media projects - and it would be a much different debate along those terms.

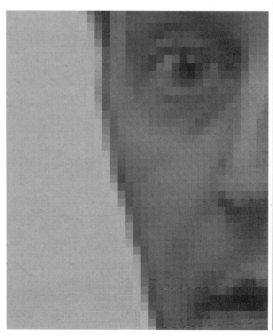

BART LOOTSMA: At the moment, there's hardly any discourse taking place regarding form and aesthetics in architecture, at the very most in the public media, where the tendency is to greatly oversimplify the field. Specifically, Bernard Hulsman from the NRC Handelsblad newspaper makes ardent and desperate attempts to warm up the corpse of postmodernism by preferring the house of Bill Gates to the architecture of NOX, for example. In the architectural world, everything revolves around organization; just think of your own VPRO building, which was designed by MVRDV. That's why I think a comparison between urban planning and media design is much more sensible than a comparison between architecture and media design, since the aesthetics of the individual building always obscure the conversation.

DICK RIJKEN: I see a parallel: can we then place architecture alongside design, and urban planning alongside communications?

BART LOOTSMA: No, it's not that easy. Even architecture revolves first and foremost around organization. Urban planning has to, by definition, be open. It has to do with processes which are completed over the course of many years, and which are therefore subject to many changing influences. Just as they do in the media, infrastructure and its accessibility play an important role here. Furthermore, within an urban planing design, the individual desires of the inhabitants have to be addressed, but they also have to be balanced against one another so that they don't get in each other's way. There are always new concepts being launched for how this process is supposed to be carried out. The developments within the media, specifically within the communications media, play an important roll in this.

LARS SPUYBROEK: Bernard Hulsman just longs for virtuality as the total replacement of life and reality by machines. In Bill Gates' Eagles Nest, his Smart House in Heimatstil, poor Bill will end up as a thousand-pound baby in the center of his still-universal power, steered by remote control, where the Things That Think will become better at remembering Bill's actions, learning them, and then DOING THEM FOR HIM. So he'll end up more virtual than Michael Jackson. We could also consider virtuality something that charges and activates reality, but then you'll need a completely different concept of machines and how they should not "fit" to us, and still engage so much in our lives that they will form an unstable aggregate, which is neither man nor machine.

NICK WEST: THERE IS A LONGING FOR SOME KIND OF GROUNDING IN CYBERSPACE

MICHAEL HENSEL: IT'S NOT CONVINCING TO SAY CYBERSPACE IS NOT A REAL SPACE BECAUSE IT IS NOT PHYSICALLY GROUNDED

DICK RIJKEN: WE'RE LIVING IN NETWORKS OF MEANING WHICH ARE GROUNDED IN MEDIA AND COMMUNICATIONS TECHNOLOGY

GREG LYNN: WHAT EXACTLY IS COMPLEXITY IF AN INFORMATION ENVIRONMENT IS MORE COMPLEX THAN A CITY

LARS SPUYBROEK: WHO'S INTERESTED IN "BEING HUMAN"? ONLY ROBOTS ARE!

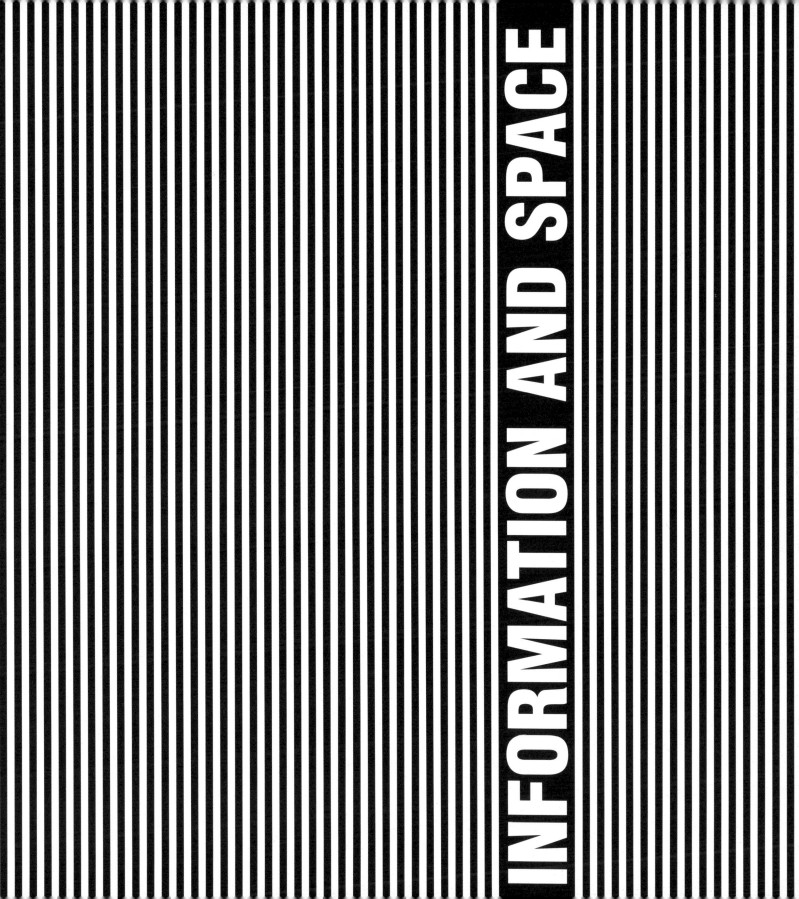

INFORMATION AND SPACE

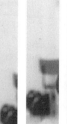

DICK RIJKEN: Information and space can be connected in various ways, a few of which I'd like to formulate here.

SPACE AS A METAPHOR

DICK RIJKEN: First of all, space in information: space as a metaphor. The WWW is swarming with virtual "rooms" and "buildings". This is supposed to be easier for the users, because they immediately see how they're supposed to navigate: "Aha, a door, that must be the exit," or "Aha, a cabinet, what could be in there?" etc. In practice, this works out horribly. The screen is flat, and the user is looking *at* it (since he's not sitting inside), the mouse runs along a surface, and the computer is often too slow for fluid 3D visualization. The result is an endless mess of interfaces used to navigate through the 3D spaces, interfaces which (at least for the time being) are slow and difficult to manage. Before you know it, the 3D spaces are full of 2D panes (in order to present text or other information that is more than happy in 2D) and we're back at square one again. I think that an architect would have designed these spaces completely differently... And why do I have to go through an entranceway when I already know exactly which room I want to reach?

BART LOOTSMA: On one hand, it's very natural that spatial metaphors borrowed from a trusted reality are used like this in designing websites. This has to do with the evolutionary phase which media designers now find themselves in. Just think of the first electric devices like lamps and tea kettles: they constantly harked back to the form that the object had when there was still a flame burning inside of it, or when it had to be set on a stove. The first steam engines had a classical design, as if they were temples. Cars originally looked like carriages. It's a delayed reaction that comes up again and again in the history of design. That it now irritates us, perhaps more so than in the past, probably comes from the fact that we've since become familiar with these kinds of evolutionary processes and now we actually want to speed them up.

For example, in both architecture and urban planning, it took a long time before people really became aware of the implications of the elevator, the automobile and the airplane. With visionaries like Frank Lloyd Wright and Le Corbusier as possible exceptions, we're actually only now getting down to it.

Perhaps this also explains that when architectural metaphors are used in programs, they're usually borrowed from a completely traditional kind of architecture in which we actually move by foot from one room to another. In buildings with an elevator, this isn't the case. There, everyone easily goes to the floor that

PHILIPPE WEGNER: What I'm looking for and still haven't found is a way for architecture to help media designers have a better understanding of what space could be. I talk about space in rather primitive terms, as in something is far away or nearby, something is to the left or to the right. For me, I would find it beneficial to think more in spatial structures.

BERT MULDER: For example, architects and media people both talk about "environments" and "space" although they mean completely different things. On the Internet, you see "worlds" and "cities" being built, and people are visiting each other in "houses". This is easy, because everyone recognizes a house. So you get a certain kind of architecture on the Internet.

LARS SPUYBROEK: Space is a metaphor in architecture, too. And there as well, it often works out horribly.

NICK WEST: The concept of grounding which exists in architecture is a concept I actually find very useful, in that our current development of new media has only very primitive concepts of space. There is a longing for some kind of grounding in cyberspace, but nobody knows how. We are fooling ourselves about cyberspace being a real place. And we're fooling ourselves about these computers being real spaces we can enter.

MICHAEL HENSEL: I don't find it convincing to say cyberspace is not a real space because it is not physically grounded.

NICK WEST: Humans want the visible space to be configured in new ways. Architecture has been too slow to keep up with that desire. So media represents the speed at which we want to go, while architecture represents the concepts we need in order to ground it properly.

NICK WEST: Media - especially new media - will have to turn to architecture for guidance whenever any term which employs physical space is used, like, for example, cyberspace or websites. Since we seem to resort to familiar three-dimensional reality for metaphors when building new constructs, the organizational principles used by architecture will become more relevant to media designers. Concerns that were previously limited to our built environment will become more and more familiar inside cyberspace. How are flows of usage organized? What defines a sense of familiarity and place? What are useful systems of navigation?

he or she has to go to, and what happens on the floors in between is irrelevant. In his book "Delirious New York", Rem Koolhaas showed that it is the elevator which allows skyscrapers to contain such an unimaginable amount of programs, programs which can be connected and recombined to each other again and again in many different ways. Some of the drawings for Constant's "Nieuw Babylon" from the sixties are collages in which fragments from different cities are assembled together because his homo ludens would be traveling by helicopter anyway. I think it's interesting that images like this have suddenly appeared in advertising campaigns for courier services, travel agencies and telecommunications firms: fragments from distant cities which, in one way or another, are directly connected with the situation "at home".

The world is presented as an archipelago of islands, with the remarkable thing being that what is supposed to lie between the islands has disappeared, or at its best is presented as empty space. That is to say that the kind of environment, such as Constant proposes or such as the elevator creates, is only now being recorded in a sort of collective consciousness. The mobile telephone has played an important role in this realization process: if you call someone on his or her mobile number, you don't first ask how he or she is doing (which used to be the case), but rather where he or she is. Perhaps the architects who discovered the

possibilities of the elevator, the car, etc. might also have a tendency to design your websites in another way. Then they'd be able to go a step further than in their other work.

DICK RIJKEN: In your story of the empty space between an archipelago's islands (yet another metaphor), we actually see that physical space has become less important for the formation of meaning. We're quickly coming to experience travel as a loss of time if the space is indeterminate, like a highway is, and we fill up this time with media: we read a book, we listen to music, or call someone up. If I'm standing on the street making a call, then I'm more "calling" than I am "standing". The street doesn't matter any more, it disappears from my field of attention.

BART LOOTSMA: Absolutely. It's for good reason that making a phone call using anything other than a hands-free system while driving an automobile has recently been forbidden.

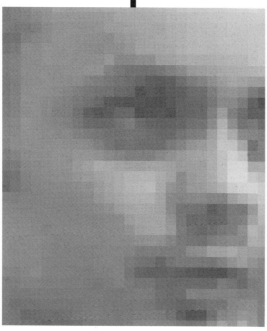

MICHAEL HENSEL: Architecture delivers the option to the new media to be submerged in matter on various scales. Potentially everything can be enabled to mediate, to issue configured information. The current research in the field of new advanced materials and intelligent materials is looking for the formation of re/active environments via the integration of matter and dataflow within one surface/spatial compound.

PLACE AS A FILTER FOR INFORMATION

DICK RIJKEN: On the other hand, there's a trend involving the fact that within the media, we're thinking more and more about the physical locations in which we could be offering content. How can we involve a person's location in the offering of information? Think about city tours, or museums where tourists can consult specific information about a specific object only when they're standing in its immediate area. The information is assembled in such a way that you actually have to stand in front of the object to understand it. Or consider the Cinema Service, which might adapt its advice to the cinema you're standing in front of. Place then becomes a filter for information.

BART LOOTSMA: Sure, Nick West gave us a nice little taste of this during the Masterclass, and in museums this kind of technology is already being widely used. West's idea was that we could all wear glasses which receive information that's broadcast from various places and buildings. I associate this with the famous photo of the cinema audience watching the 3-D film with their little white glasses, a bit ridiculous but also a bit scary. It also reminds me of the Terminator and Robocop, who were also equipped with similar gear. It's interesting that in the last film, Robocop actually became a bit more human after he had (single-handedly) unscrewed his helmet: that naked head, helplessly attached to an exoskeleton. As I've said before, I hope it doesn't come to the point where people become totally dependent on this kind of technology and on the content which this technology allows them to select, but rather that they're also trained to go through life as independent beings. This is not only a question of developing interactive programming, but of letting people have the freedom to feel things, to find them out and think about them themselves.

DICK RIJKEN: Are you bothered by the fact that the information is hyperlocal, or that its delivery involves wearing glasses? If I can see the information on my watch, does it then cease to be "ridiculous" and "scary"? Did Robocop become more human because you could see his skin, or because he had finally realized what had happened to him, who he was and who he used to be? By the way, why was he such a tragic figure? Because of the technology he had on board, or because of the value system that laid the foundation for the way his technology was programmed? Regardless of that, getting all dramatic about becoming dependent on technology is a lost cause. Our lives and our ideas are largely formed by the existence of technology. And I'm not only talking about media, but

PHILIPPE WEGNER: Media are still very much standing on their own: media have their own devices through which information reaches you. I would like to see media more embedded in the space around me. Not only in my personal space (like clothing and jewelry), but also in furniture, for example. When I look at my own living space, I see no connection between the electronic media and the hardware world. This makes it impossible to incorporate media in the way you really want to. Your house becomes more of your own cocoon the longer you live in it. The carriers of electronic media are in no way connected to that.

BRUNO FELIX: It's rather a strange paradox we have here: on one hand, it seems interesting to connect certain information to certain places. On the other hand, media and its corresponding distribution channels and playback devices are becoming increasingly smaller, more portable and more personal. These developments mean that it is becoming increasingly easy to use media to transform any given place into, for example, a workplace (with a laptop), a private communication space (with a cellular phone), or a relaxation space (with a walkman). This ultimately results in the demand for more and more multi-application spaces (like the VPRO building). So the difference is in the function that a particular space has, and the function that a person can give to it.

LARS SPUYBROEK: Who's interested in "being human"? Only robots are!

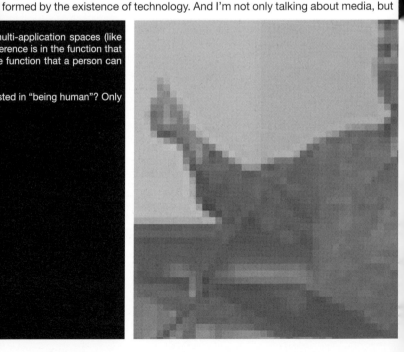

also transportation, electricity, medical technology, and last but not least, architectural technology.

BART LOOTSMA: I wouldn't want to play it up that heavily, but I think it has to do with the whole constellation of the glasses, the broadcasters, and the type and quality of the information. I still maintain, and I know it's terribly naive, another dream which just as much uses technology as its foundation, but one in which the technology might one day make it possible for us to attain a paradisiacal state where we can all once again go through life naked in a clean environment. I think that this secret longing also lurks just as strongly behind most architectural and medical technology. With media, there's something at hand in terms of people's uncontrollable urge to communicate, or more exactly: the urge to make oneself comprehensible and to express something different. There's so often a bit too much ambition in this that it makes me embarrassed. But nonetheless, of course the question is to what degree all of these glasses will be the same, interactive or not. The difference between the watch and the glasses is that the watch is more non-committal. But you're right, even though you're setting the stakes high. Of course we've been living for a long time in a technotope, and not in a biotope. And we've since all become cyborgs, as Karin Spaink rightly says

in her introduction to Donna Haraway's "A Cyborg Manifesto": we take medicine, have transplants and prostheses (and not only when we're sick), we have countless machines that are very close to our bodies, or even inside of them, which replace, increase and expand the functions of these things; we are seamlessly surrounded by cars and airplanes in which an artificial climate rules, just as it does in the buildings we produce. "There's not very much to be found that's 'natural' about our bodies. Or more exactly: the border between nature and culture, between one's self and the exterior, between inherent and received, between gift and self-contribution, is diffuse. We have outgrown the stage of mere flesh and blood. Perhaps we now consist of flesh, tissue, texts and chips, of blood, bytes and data networks."

Our bodies and our environment are largely manufacturable, and we want to know this, too. The most fantastic mythological figure of the nineties is neither the Terminator nor Robocop, but the more advanced Terminator 2, who is made of a kind of liquid memory material which can assume any desired form and identity: man, woman, and fighting machine, self-repairing after having been shot to shreds. Here, the ultimate longings of the transsexual and the body-builder come together. But we don't have to come to the point of having ears sewed onto us by technology (as Stelarc is literally planning to do, by the way).

NICK WEST: It's important to think of the possible construct of a "neighborhood web" as not being limited to broadcasters sending advertisements to consumers. It could just as easily be authors communicating with readers, or game players talking with each other, or any combination of guides, histories, poetry, interactive tournaments, rants, photo essays, musical accompaniment, anything. The point is to imagine physical space being opened up to a thousand different simultaneous, overlapping annotations. I share the distaste for excessive gadgetry. But gadgets tend to become invisible over time, like watches and Walkmans. And the ultimate challenge is to find a way of embedding our cultural intelligence inside the built environment so that it becomes perceptible to as many people as possible. That's where we need the help of architects.

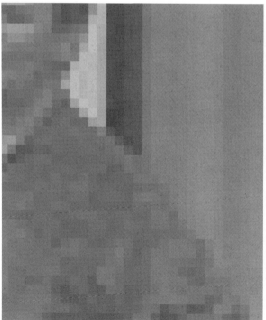

48

Just as we've always painstakingly considered how we deal with nature and with our fellow human beings, we also have to be critical in learning how to deal with this second nature. This isn't the same as a rearguard action against it. It's for good reason that over the past few years, the image of the sailor disappearing into a whirlpool has been used frequently. Edgar Allen Poe used it long ago in his story "A Descent Into the Maelstrom". After first uselessly putting up a fight, the sailor gives in and discovers that there are regularities in the whirlpool's behavior. And thus he ultimately manages to save himself. Analogous to this, Marshall McLuhan pleaded in "Understanding Media" that multimedia installations like those developed by artists in the sixties could learn us how to deal with the bombardment of "our extended faculties". According to him, we should learn like boxers "to ride with the punch instead of taking it on the chin". In "The Fatal Strategies", Baudrillard proposed that we might have to battle the obscenity with our own means. He's also interested in everything with the prefix "trans". These kinds of lines of reasoning interest me more than the possibilities of launching new gadgets: this is indeed happening, and I can see it coming. The interesting thing about Robocop is that he has to assume the form of technology in order to fight technology. When he stands with his visor open, he becomes more human, but also more vulnerable. His naked face and eyes become visible again.

DICK RIJKEN: I'm getting a bit tired of the fact that you keep suggesting that media designers don't think people can think for themselves. While designing media, we take the user very seriously. Your arguments against the dependence on technology imply that we should actually do away with education, and that everyone has to discover everything on their own. And most of all, never let a guide take you anywhere. Or does it perhaps have to do with the guides themselves, and where they stand? What is the VPRO if not a guide? It's not the fact that you teach, it's what you teach. I'm very excited about taking my audience seriously and giving them resources for reflection. And what's more, interactive media facilitate dialogical communication.

BART LOOTSMA: I think my reservation is primarily inspired by the pushy character of many media. Offering information, which you were discussing in your question, is not per se interactive. And if it is interactive, then who takes the initiative for the interactivity, and how broad is it? Does the interactivity also allow for things that the designer and his or her client are less interested in, or which they simply haven't thought about? Microsoft has recently, without asking me, replaced my Internet provider's homepage with one of its own interactive sites, in which I can download everything from their product range if I want to. That's

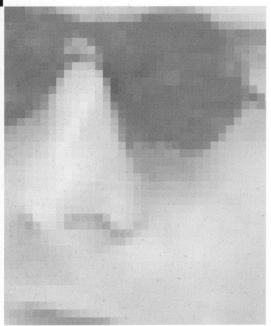

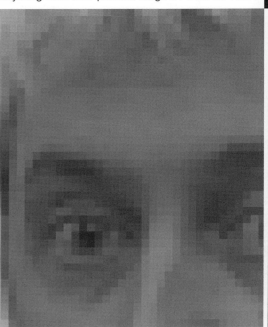

all I am allowed to want, and it turns out to be difficult to get rid of this shit and get my provider's own homepage back.
I think that there's a difference (or should be) between education and advertising or propaganda. Maybe that's also a difference between us both, regardless of the fact that I'm more involved with architecture than you are, and that you're more involved with media: I'm a critic, theoretician and teacher, and you work at an communication consultancy, for the broadcasting field, and teach as well. I have a greater need to see the whole thing from more of a distance, and from a more academic viewpoint.

DICK RIJKEN: Reflection from the trenches... May I make one last attempt here (by means of yet another metaphor)? What's the best birthday present? I would say it's the present that is at once typical OF the giver and typical FOR the person whose birthday it is. If I know you well enough, I can give you something that is even more than what you asked for. This is the dimension that the media are going to be experimenting with in the upcoming years.

BART LOOTSMA: The largest section of the market has nothing whatsoever to do with birthday presents, and the information that is fired at us by retailers in Nick

West's example even less. But nonetheless, of course I think it's agreeable, as well as good, if the production machines are changed in such a way that products better meet my own specific wishes.

DICK RIJKEN: If place is a filter for information, will places then be battling for attention? Will there then be a greater demand for architects who can design buildings as attention-getters? Will we then employ superlocal media in order to tell a story together with a building? Are stories WITH buildings nicer than stories WITHOUT them?

BART LOOTSMA: Places have already been striving for attention for a long time, and the media have long been instrumental in this. That's what my lecture "The New Landscape" was about, which I also gave in abbreviated form during the Masterclass. In the city, various bars and cinemas battle each other for attention, but offices along the highways do as well. On a larger scale, various cities and regions battle for attention. It was for good reason that Frankfurt and Rotterdam made large-scale investments a few years ago in their cultural infrastructure (museums, theaters and cinemas). That was to make it more attractive for businesses to settle there. The same holds true for the gigantic multifunc-

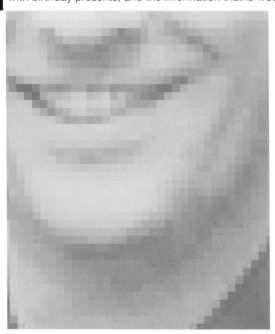

Bart Lootsma: Where we want to go in a city only depends on the specific quality and the amount of Stim a place has to offer us ("Stim" is a term introduced by Lars Lerup. It comes from stimulation, as William Gibson uses it in his novel "Mona Lisa Overdrive", where "stims" are a kind of mixture between the soap series we know from television and virtual reality. In other books in the "Neuromancer" cycle, Gibson uses the term "simstim", which is even more linked to computer technology, and which makes the stim even more artificial, "simulated"). Where we go has nothing to do whether the place is public, semi-public or private. On the contrary, semi-public spaces like bars, restaurants, discos and shopping malls have gained in importance in the city. In larger cities, complex semi-public networks grow, networks that are used in the same way we zap through the different television stations. We use them intuitively and we are easily bored, constantly hunting for new, possibly even stronger experiences. "It's cool or it sucks", in the MTV terminology of Beavis and Butthead.
The bars and discotheques which Alfredo Arribas successfully realized in Barcelona are the perfect illustration of this tendency. The interior of "Network", a strange hybrid

between hamburger joint, serious restaurant, bar, pool room, and discotheque is inspired by the Ridley Scott movie "Blade Runner". Another of his creations, "Velvet", a mixture between nightclub, bar and disco, is inspired by David Lynch's "Blue Velvet". The latter was so successful that a much larger version of it has now been realized in an industrial area on the periphery. (extract from unpublished manuscript "The New Landscape")

tional stadiums which are rising up from the ground everywhere, with the help of local municipalities. They are inextricably bound to both local as well as international media networks and events such as the Europacup and the World Championships, and bound to media multinationals like the Rolling Stones and the Spice Girls. Having architects design buildings which are attention-getters themselves was largely a phenomenon of the eighties and the beginning of the nineties, when every city had to have a Meier, a Rossi, a Graves or at least a Mendini: a building made by an architect who had himself become a star in the international media circus of architecture. I get the idea that there's now a tendency to think more directly in terms of networks and programs, a tendency in which such externally striking architecture is no longer as necessary.

DICK RIJKEN: Does that then mean that this kind of architecture requires all kinds of media to give form to the programs and to communicate? If so, then we're talking once again about media tied to a particular place. With or without glasses...

BART LOOTSMA: Sure, of course. Science fiction author William Gibson once wrote that cyberspace looks like Los Angeles at night, seen from five thousand feet in the air. The opposite is perhaps even more true, but in any case the two things touch one another and are fused together. But if we're per se discussing media tied to a particular place, I don't know if you have to consider it in those terms. The dislocation Gibson introduces when he talks of an image seen from the air seems important to me (satellites?), just as does the connection between individual buildings and other spaces, virtual or real. I think that the buildings themselves are becoming externally cooler because there are so many influences being fired at us. I could also corroborate this with examples.

SPACE MADE OF INFORMATION

DICK RIJKEN: As a second angle of incidence from which we can consider space and information, I want to discuss space made of information: virtual reality. In this case, a user settles thoroughly INTO a space, preferably by means of a stereoscopic projection. More and more, computer games take place in 3D worlds. Who designs these worlds? Wipeout 2097 (Sony Playstation, PC), for example, is a futuristic racing game in which the player whirls across various racetracks in so-called "anti-gravity" vehicles at staggering speeds, in competition with a number of other players. Or Doom, the renowned massacre game,

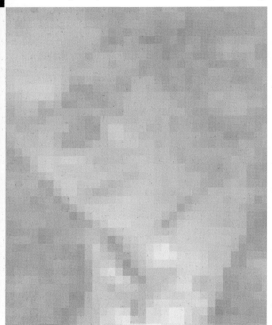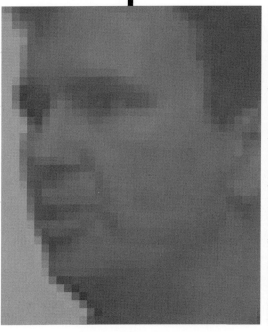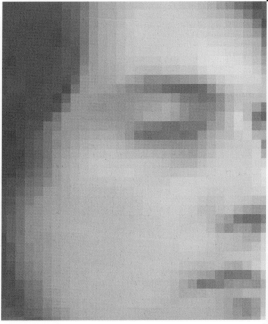

which also takes place completely in 3D. In these kinds of games, the quality of the spatial design is a crucial factor. In this sort of application, a deep understanding of space in relation to dynamics and movement is an indispensable design quality. To what degree do these kinds of new worlds play a role in the development of spatial design in architecture?

BART LOOTSMA: I still don't immediately see the difference between the issues raised by your previous point, except for the fact that the higher reality content and the better representation of reality mean that you can move through the spaces at high speeds. Yet I can't shake the impression that this has more to do with technological innovations in the computer itself than with a content-based innovation of the spatial concept. In fact, the experience of moving through entryways and tunnels is even more emphasized than it is in the navigation programs you mentioned before, furnished with doors and trapdoors behind which it seems Alice in Wonderland is hiding in another world.

If you ask me how these kinds of new worlds play a role in architecture, then in everyday life I have to think about how a person moves through airports: from one tube to another, and then at a given moment you're standing with your eyes blinking from the light in a completely different world. In a city with an expansive and significant subway network, like Paris or Hong Kong, you have a similar kind of experience. In his novels, William Gibson has convincingly extrapolated this picture to the future. You get the feeling that his protagonists find themselves within a kind of endless network of pneumatic dispatches.

In the official history of architecture, of course we had the Metabolists, who at the beginning of the sixties designed large-scale cities on the basis of this idea, cities in which vertical buildings consisting of clusters of individual cells were to be connected by extensive networks of arterial roads. But the dominantly present arterial roads weren't goals in and of themselves, like in a computer game, but rather were necessary to bridge distances. If we're purely talking about the experience, then perhaps the H2O pavilion by NOX and Kas Oosterhuis comes the closest to a computer game, because it is a house in which visitors experience an adventure as they move through it, an adventure they can even influence to a certain degree. But in general, of course architecture is about much more than providing experiences. Architecture and urban planning, above all, have to accommodate and organize life itself. "Entertainment" certainly plays an ever more important role in this, for example in shopping malls and theme parks, but these remain the cream of the crop, and anyway they're extremely transitory. In Los Angeles, I recently visited the Jon Jerde Partnership, a firm which

GREG LYNN: We architects look towards media for new techniques of working, for ways of rethinking the profession, discovering new spatial models, new forms of display and communication. As an educator, I have the experience of seeing a third of my students going to Hollywood and working on films. Some of them went to work as art directors on "Judge Dredd". I remember saying, "You really have to take the experimental design methods and use the film 'Judge Dredd' as a vehicle. You should try and work experimentally in film." They were killed. The producers said, "We don't want you to think, we know what we want, we've tested it." It turns out that they were the most antagonistic people you could find. So, my experience is that architects are hungry for new concepts and for transgressions. But media designers, because it's a new discipline, need some conservatory aspects.

BERT MULDER: The media not only change the physical walls of a house, but they're also making me think about architecture in a different way. Of course home and garden magazines have been around for a long time now, but you have to go out and buy them, and they have a much different circulation impact than television does. On TV, I see home-repair programs where all kinds of houses are built and renovated, and then I think, "I want that, too". In the 50s people also spent a lot of time on their own curtains and pillowcases, but back then they had to make them themselves and would spend a thousand years on them. You bought a bed when you were young and you could be very proud if you died in that same bed. Nowadays you compose a different house every season, and everyone consumes themselves silly. Thus media changes the ideas that people have in regard to architecture. You also see this with companies that have very special buildings designed only because of the grand aura that this generates in the media. It's very alluring to use the exterior of a building to foster recognition and to tell something about your organization. An advertising agency in California, for example, recently built a four-story high telescope as their office. It has noth-

designs huge shopping malls all over the world. In the Netherlands, they designed the "Koopgoot" in Rotterdam, a little one. They increasingly make their designs so that they can be completely restyled every five to ten years, in order to allow new media to play an increasingly important role. Otherwise the public starts to get bored and the project inevitably loses its appeal. Projects like these seem as if they're a stage or a TV screen that can be reprogrammed again and again. In Las Vegas, they literally covered Fremont Street with this kind of screen, hundreds of meters long, on which a different program is played every hour at night. Aesthetically, the richer formal vocabulary that architects can use because of CAD-CAM is just one of the possible effects of the computer. In a completely different way it is the flow of images that has become available through the media that provokes the desire for a new aesthetics. After techniques like montage and collage, mediating techniques, morphing and simulation programmes present new possibilities to generate forms. And maybe, as Rem Koolhaas suggested to me in an interview I did with him for DOMUS magazine, it will be the media themselves that will completely take over the aesthetical part of architecture, as a changeabele, temporary atmosphere, liberating the architect to concentrate on the essence of his profession: organizing space.

DICK RIJKEN: Then does this mean the end of architecture as an art form? Are buildings themselves being transformed into infrastructures for media, like the network connections of the Internet or the printing presses of newspapers? What kind of designers will we need for designing the new spatial programs? Will they be communications strategists? Product managers? Graphic designers? Architects? Urban planners? Retailers?

BART LOOTSMA: At the moment, as opposed to at the beginning of the eighties, I don't find the question of whether architecture is an art form to be terribly interesting. Even back then I thought that the content of art had changed in such a way that you could no longer talk exclusively about generating images, and that's even more strongly the case now. Rather it was about developing cultural concepts. This broadening of a discipline I used as an example for architecture. Architecture has to consider this example, because of the fact that it no longer has a self-evident tradition. Thus, just like art, architecture has to continually develop concepts in order to keep up with the development of culture. In this sense, then, it has been relegated or condemned to art. The borders of the disciplines have since been almost definitively dissolved. They only continue to exist in legislation. The internally delineating role of the disciplines has thus been

ing to do with the question of whether or not such a telescope is functional or tenable as an office; it just looks good.

GREG LYNN: There are already places where architecture and media are merging together intensively. If an architect is designing a shopping mall in America, he also has to do a multiplex movie theatre and some kind of amusement park. They also deal intensively with visual culture of a type that is like television in terms of billboards, advertisements, and placing kiosks in the space. For example, most malls have Walt Disney or Warner Brother branch stores in them. And a casino developer recently told me that banks won't fund a new casino unless it has a minimum of seven virtual reality rides. They also deal with bringing entertainers to the space, for example in Planet Hollywood and on 42nd street in New York. These places are totally developed to be virtual theme environments. I see that entertainment and Internet strategies for films, television and architecture have melted into a kind of single composite, a mutation between a theme park, a mall, a casino. These are strange hybrids, but those are the places where it has been tested. Most

other institutions, like colleges, museums and houses are not ready for that kind of merging yet, because they want to keep things very discrete.

PHILIPPE WEGNER: The media will take over more than just the aesthetic domain. With respect to infrastructures or technological innovations and their impact on society as a whole and the relationship to cultural differences, changes do not always come gradually. Sometimes new things are picked up quickly and lead to an avalanche of changes. Other abrupt changes take place because a critical border is crossed. Take our highways. Combined with affordable communication infrastructures and devices, there are now more options than working in the office, which leads to major impacts on family life, etc.

LARS SPUYBROEK: There are now two movements in architecture. One is to push architecture down into the domain of urbanism, the programmatic field, the support of media-/events. All architecture, in this view, should retreat, and the only thing one should concentrate on as a designer is the floor, and anything on the floor consequently becomes a

quote: either it is chosen from a catalogue (the columns and the walls just as much as the furniture) or has been designed by a minor architect (often working at the same office). The other movement is to have architecture move up, more in the direction of furniture, the mobile, the moveable, textile, even towards more flexible material like media. Obviously I'm in the last category, and I very much resist the distinction between Media and Architecture, between service and served, between shell and events, between tectonics and textile. I start by creating events in the structure necessarily made up of Soft Matter.

GREG LYNN: Just as the Internet has increased the sales of books in the US, I doubt that media will end architecture. The design of material objects has been increasing exponentially for some time, and I expect that this will not only continue, but that the latest manifestation has now become digital media.

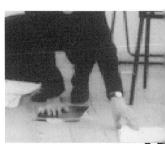

overtaken by the general legal, bureaucratic and technocratic "Abstract Systems" that sociologist Anthony Giddens discusses. The designers of new spatial programs have already largely become the kind of people you mentioned above, perhaps even predominantly so. And they've always been doing it, by the way.

DICK RIJKEN: The difference between my two kinds of perspectives regarding 3D visualisations exists in the difference between the space as a means (the spatial metaphor) and the space as a goal (virtual reality). This is clearly about the offering of a spatial experience as such, and not about the presentation of information. No WIPEOUT without cool race tracks, no DOOM without those eerie dungeons. How good are architects at actually designing fantasy worlds?

BART LOOTSMA: Of course virtual reality is very interesting, for various reasons. First of all, because it involves a potential multiplication of space with a transient character, which offers tremendous perspectives regarding freedom. And secondly, because an actual, true-to-life replica of another space somewhere far away, in combination with robots controlled from the site of replica, enables people to take actions in other places while not actually having to be physically present. This might mean that people can securely remain working from home, and that they may need to travel less.

But anyway, architects are indeed very good at designing fantasy worlds. Most of these games are designed by architects. Most of the architects who Greg Lynn educates in his Paperless Studio at Columbia University then go off to work in Hollywood; it pays much better and you don't get any mud on your shoes. Lebbeus Woods is also very popular there. I recently had this same discussion with Rene Daalder, a Dutch filmmaker in Hollywood and a pioneer of computer-generated special effects and completely computer-generated environments. For his film "Habitat", he developed the first completely virtual house. He has a state of the art computer lab where only architects work. At the moment he's working on a film, "Strawberry Fields", which is based on 41 Beatles songs. It will be a musical which takes place completely in a science fiction world with completely virtual architecture. The theme of the film is the relationship between virtual and actual reality, and it assumes the form of a battle between the powers-that-be and terrorists who blow up an electrical power station, for example. What's interesting is that Daalder used to make films with Rem Koolhaas, and that they both still have a lot of respect for each other's ways of thinking. Yet Daalder doesn't understand Koolhaas' architecture because for

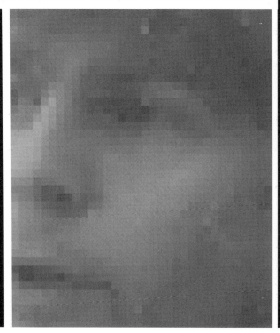

GREG LYNN: In my studio, 26 students work exclusively on computers, and last year I had six students leaving architecture school for Hollywood, doing dancing shampoo bottles and dinosaurs for "Jurassic Park" or computer models for "Judge Dredd". The electronic media from Hollywood often look for architects, especially for 3D environments. The sad thing is that the architects didn't do anything different than anybody else would have. I would like to think that architecture transmits more into the media than just technical knowledge, but so far there hasn't been a big shift. It will depend on a new generation of architects and new media designers.

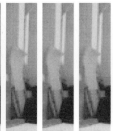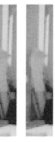

him it doesn't offer any attractive visual experience. I personally think that Rem Koolhaas is doing exactly what you're asking for, namely offering a spatial experience and not unlocking information. Yet it's the fact that the experience goes down a few extra layers of information that makes it not a cave or a fairy tale castle, but rather a building in which people are taken seriously. People other than the architect himself can add more information to it. So it has a much more open structure than your simple computer games do.

DICK RIJKEN: But what else interferes with the daily course of events like the spatial experience? I hear from users of Koolhaas' Educatorium at the Rijksuniversiteit in Utrecht that they find it a "true building for architects". They see that exciting things are happening spatially, but the building really starts to get on their nerves when they have to have lunch there, take courses there and do exams there (every day). Is that taking people seriously?

BART LOOTSMA: If there's anything that gets on one's nerves, then perhaps it's the fairy-tale castle aspects of the building's decoration: the ceiling and wallpaper. Although I do find it beautiful, it's ultimately fleeting and replaceable. But that's not the essence of the building. The essence is that your friends now have

a place where they can have lunch, etc., and that it's organized so that several buildings and groups of scientists can seamlessly be connected. It's a kind of "server" actually.

DICK RIJKEN: My argument goes a bit further than "simple computer games". A central element of virtual reality is the (literal) position of the user. Am I looking at spaces from the outside, or am I inside of them? This distinction is more than simply technical, and it doesn't necessarily have to be limited to entertainment. At the moment there is fervent experimentation being conducted with 3D visualizations of complex databases, where the user is located INSIDE of them. I've seen applications where the user can proceed through a sea of stock market quotes with a virtual reality set on his or her head, which is really much different than looking at graphics or animations. What's remarkable is that the better examples are of a fairly abstract nature; there's no attempt made whatsoever to imitate familiar objects or spaces. I think it would be very interesting to have architects, with their feel for 3D spaces, think about complex games or visualizations.

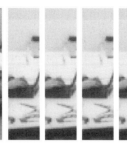

SPACE CREATED BY INFORMATION

DICK RIJKEN: The third point is the space that is created by information: the information environment. It is a less literal metaphor, which aims at (often open) constellations of various information and communications products. The average PC (connected to a network) is an information environment: a collection of programs and files which the user, as an acting and navigating subject, forms a part of. But we can also see television and newspapers as information spaces. Many information systems have a structure which is experienced as an environment, with differences between "here" and "there" and different connections between the "spaces". But significantly, without needing to make use of 3D visualizations. I think architecture can feed the discourse regarding these kinds of information spaces. The user creates an "experience" while he proceeds through an information environment. There is not any single route; instead there is the potential for many possible paths or actions. This makes me think of how a building doesn't need to force a single specific route, but rather a number of routes which the physical space can enable. Although an architect doesn't develop one route specifically, he does make design decisions that ultimately determine the possible experiences. The space then works as a process facili-

tator. The emphasis on "experience" as the dynamic result of a design seems to me something that architects, and especially urban planners, need to recognize.

BART LOOTSMA: I agree with the first part of your argument. The way in which the user uses his PC and television is absolutely comparable with how he moves through the city. We get easily bored and want to zap between intense experiences. Furthermore, cities are getting more and more vast, and we make very selective use of them, just as we only take in some of the information which the space flings at us. But I wouldn't want to see the "experience" as the guideline; that's only a goal if we're looking for entertainment. Perhaps we, as we are being shown the way through a more or less traditional European city, have a series of experiences in the form of landmarks which serve as orientation points. But if we're talking about a vast and complex metropolis like Tokyo or Los Angeles, this does not work anymore. There we have to trust in more abstract systems of navigation, maps and sign-posting for example. Newspapers, radio, television and the telephone make us aware of where we have to be for specific programs and experiences. And here, the new telecommunications media based on satellite navigation should help us out anew. I'm convinced that specifically this last item will bring about a true revolution in urban planning, the results of which still

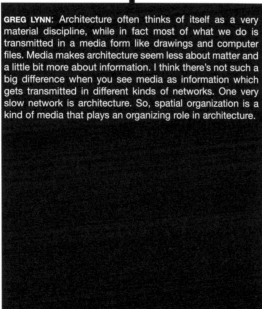

GREG LYNN: Architecture often thinks of itself as a very material discipline, while in fact most of what we do is transmitted in a media form like drawings and computer files. Media makes architecture seem less about matter and a little bit more about information. I think there's not such a big difference when you see media as information which gets transmitted in different kinds of networks. One very slow network is architecture. So, spatial organization is a kind of media that plays an organizing role in architecture.

56

can't be seen in their entirety. If you're talking about the space as a process facilitator, then I don't think as much of experiences as I do of processes of urbanization. How can a design or structure accommodate and organize these processes? In this field, urban planning contains a wealth of experience. But once again there are high expectations of computer technology, namely in regard to potentially simulating these kind of processes. I think that's why in architecture and urban planning circles there's more interest in computer games like SimCity and artificial life than there is in the games we were talking about before. Perhaps an insight into these sorts of processes could lead to new forms of navigation in the urban and information environments, which just keep growing and growing. It's no longer just about navigation in a static sense, but rather within a constantly growing and mobile whole.

DICK RIJKEN: I envision "experience" as being broader than simply entertainment. For me, experience also has to do with understanding the stress that reigns in a production department the day before a deadline. Or with the reassurance of a consumer who, one minute after he's bought something on the Internet, receives an e-mail message with a clear description of the transaction and its financial consequences. Or with first-time visitors that find their way in a

complex city by using media for guidance. The alienation that overtakes you in such a city is an "experience". Understanding this is very helpful in designing all kinds of media. And this applies, it seems to me, to a lot of architecture as well.

BART LOOTSMA: Sure, but because the information environment quickly becomes more complex than the city, urban planing will not be able to help media designers on the basis of traditional experience, I'm afraid.

DICK RIJKEN: So then we have two fields throwing their hands up in the air, which isn't all that pleasant. I've been bothered for years by the absolute lack of attention in the world of digital media paid to this more complex level of consideration: everyone always talks about the functionality and aesthetics of components (an individual word processor, a spreadsheet or a website) while our actions mostly take place in information environments with many components which could all actively fit alongside one other. We hardly have any models for contemplating the qualities of these kinds of environments, in contrast to the often carefully delimited functions of the "components". How do urban planners think about the qualities or cultures of cities? That's part of the solution...

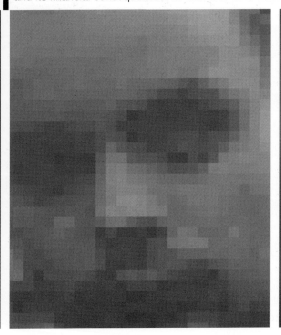

GREG LYNN: What exactly is complexity if an information environment is more complex than a city? Why do these kinds of discussions seem to produce these types of unfounded factoids all the time? What is at stake for information networks in being more complex than a city if such a statement were true?

PHILIPPE WEGNER: Isn't this complexity what might be the common ground between architecture, urban planning, industrial design and media design? Things can't be covered as separate entities, and traditional experiences can't provide a stable basis. There's no choice but to stick together.

   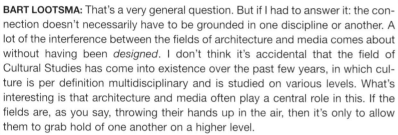

BART LOOTSMA: That's a very general question. But if I had to answer it: the connection doesn't necessarily have to be grounded in one discipline or another. A lot of the interference between the fields of architecture and media comes about without having been *designed*. I don't think it's accidental that the field of Cultural Studies has come into existence over the past few years, in which culture is per definition multidisciplinary and is studied on various levels. What's interesting is that architecture and media often play a central role in this. If the fields are, as you say, throwing their hands up in the air, then it's only to allow them to grab hold of one another on a higher level.

SPACE AS INFORMATION

DICK RIJKEN: As a fourth angle of consideration we have space as information: the readable space. In what ways is the space itself a bearer of meaning? In and of itself, this is nothing new. Buildings have always been representations of ideas. But thinking back to our remarks on the computer as a "pluralism machine", in what ways is the pluralism of our culture currently being translated by architects and urban planners in their designs? If, in an information society, the meaning of things becomes more important than the things themselves,

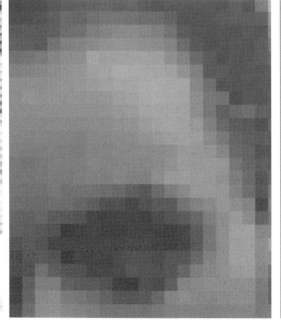 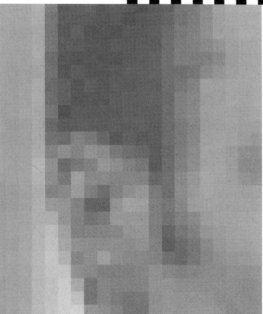 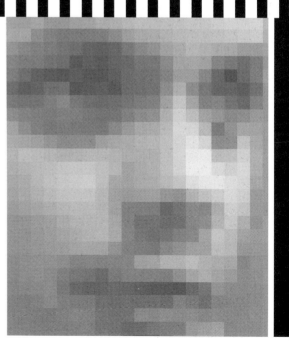

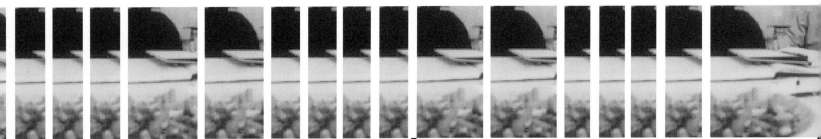

then what happens with buildings? We're already seeing that people are looking on a grand scale for new paradigms for the formation of meaning. Recent research in the Netherlands shows that the church isn't doing well, but that there is a growing interest in spirituality. New Age is a perfect example: a pluralistic converging of many ideas and rituals for making meaning. Does this also hold true for architecture? I can remember that Greg Lynn complained about the fact there are more books to be found in bookstores these days about Feng Shui (an Eastern approach to space and building in which flows of energy play a central role in how space is considered) than there are about Western architecture.

BART LOOTSMA: The architectural space isn't just a bearer of meaning itself, but it helps facilitate the generation of the meanings which are determined within it. And perhaps it excludes one meaning, or is at odds with another one. In this context, I'd like to quote the text from an "advertisement for architecture" by architect Bernard Tschumi from 1978: "TO REALLY APPRECIATE ARCHITEC-TURE, YOU MAY EVEN NEED TO COMMIT A MURDER. Architecture is defined by the actions it witnesses as much as by the enclosure of its walls. Murder in the Street differs from Murder in the Cathedral in the same way as Love in the Street differs from the Street of Love. Radically".

If we're talking about facilitating a pluralistic culture, then architects and especially urban planners have already long been working on this, of course. Think in your neighborhood of the VPRO building by MVRDV, which is a kind of landscape containing the idea that the inhabitants can design their own space with furniture and other attributes they've brought in themselves. In another design for an apartment building in Berlin, which first made MVRDV famous, they filled the volume of an apartment building (like in the computer game Tetris) with as many different apartments as possible. The often remarkable forms of the apartments make the inhabitants constantly aware of their neighbors, whose apartments thus have to be different than their own.

So over the course of time, there have been many concepts developed which have attempted to generate a pluriform society, from Frank Lloyd Wright's Broadacre City and Le Corbusier's Plan Obus to the concepts of Habraken and the SAR in the Netherlands (based on participation in the individual floor plans within a support structure), from Herman Hertzberger (the Centraal Beheer (Central Administration) office building) to the anarchistic proposals of Lucien Kroll. Of course, the requisite problems cling to (or until recently clung to) these kinds of approaches. Thus the first inhabitants in most of these concepts usually establish the form of an apartment, while no one said that it would be right for

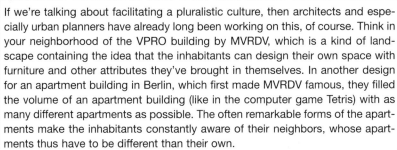

BERT MULDER: My prediction is that if architecture and media are going to become integrated over the next couple of years, architecture will be confronted with the "meaning" side, with the psychological side. What we're doing compels us to ask existential questions.

There are many forces of order on the physical side, the aesthetic side, and the psychological side. There is also a universal order that comes from a completely different domain, one we don't know in the Western sciences, because our eyes are turned towards matter. All of the other cultures on earth have a view of the world where higher values and physical values mesh, where the order of the universe, of a city and of a person intersect. When the architectural field is confronted with a more psychological order, with the fact that in the transition to the twenty-first century we need a more integrated, synergetic feel for ourselves, architecture will then also be confronted with completely new and forgotten kinds of order which come from this universal kind of thinking.

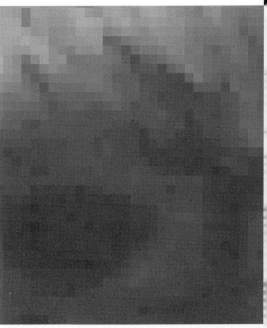

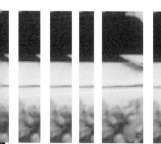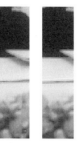

the next inhabitants. Good-bye progress, especially in light of our increasing proclivity to move house. Furthermore, the pluriformity is usually realized by one firm, with one method of construction; the pluriformity then becomes, to a certain degree, a sham. Carel Weeber specifically fulminated in the Netherlands against this kind of hypocrisy, and although his standpoint might not be so popular outside of architectural circles, I used to agree with him on many points. Perhaps then it's more understandable and more honest to generate apartments which are as neutral as possible.

In his "In Holland staat een huis" ("In Holland there is a House") project of 1995, Adriaan Geuze shed light on another problem in designers' own striving for pluriformity. In it, he convincingly demonstrated with photographic reports from recent districts and a large model of 1,000,000 small houses (the amount we want to build in the Netherlands by 2015) that it is precisely the striving for individual pluriformity which leads to frightening monotony, because the individuality is swallowed up by the larger whole. Or look at the pathetic villa districts which are slowly popping up everywhere in the Netherlands and which are already being compared to scary diseases.

I would have absolutely no answer to the question of whether the formation of meaning has anything to do with spirituality. That is, to recall Wittgenstein, a senseless question. In regard to Feng Shui, that's more your hobbyhorse than Greg's, although his friend Bernard Cache also discusses it in his readings, in regard to computers. But Cache isn't so much interested in Asian culture from the viewpoint of the creation of meaning, but rather because according to him there is a longer and more refined tradition in the area of abstract thinking. That's something else. During my trip to Asia with the Fund for Visual Arts, Design and Architecture last autumn, we asked about Feng Shui everywhere. The ridiculous and ashamed answer was usually that in some cases (all of which were unofficial) it was indeed taken into account (with hilarious results) because the rich investors were often very old and from another generation. Regardless of that, it seemed that Feng Shui could be negotiated. If there's one thing to be learned from the Asians, it's the fact the true formation of meaning these days lies in numbers: the amount of people, homes, products and traffic that they cause in relation to the economy. The computer networks in which all this data sing and chant are the real churches of today, already. The rituals of the market have ousted those of the church. In Singapore, which in religious terms is actually a fairly pluriform society, religious buildings have the shortest long-lease period of all existing urban planning categories.

BERT MULDER: What I find interesting about Feng Shui is the fact that as a whole, it's a statement in a different cosmology, where "force" and "energy" blend with material, land, and personal existence. It always makes me adjust my Western scientific view and serves as a source of reflection, forcing me to go beyond functional, structural, aesthetic or economic viewpoints. The fact that it is practiced more in the West than in the East (as are Indian mediation practices, shamanistic rituals and Muslim mysticism) is more exemplary of an increasingly global multi-culturalism than it is of a strong argument for its meaninglessness. Feng Shui is interesting precisely because it is meaningless in the current paradigm. The question is not about Feng Shui, but about the paradigm: how do we out-think ourselves?

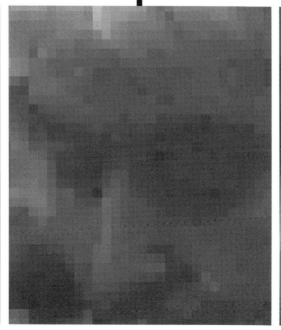

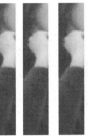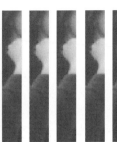

DICK RIJKEN: "Where our language suggests a body and there is none: there, we should like to say, is a spirit" (Ludwig Wittgenstein, Philosophical Investigations, No. 36). The first person who was confused by Wittgenstein's thinking was Wittgenstein himself. If there was someone who eventually came to the discovery that every use of language is rooted in situations, then it was him... For many people, spirituality is very much a means of creating meaning that doesn't necessarily have anything to do with traditional or fundamental religion. As I've already said, churches are losing ground and hordes of people are rightly searching for new forms.

But my point has more to do with creating meaning than with spirituality. The image that your remarks conjure up is one of an international capitalism in its most terrifying form. Yet I can still hope that architects will assume their responsibility, and won't look for meaning in numbers. Precisely because architecture, as you've formulated it yourself, helps facilitate the generation of meanings which are determined within it, thereby excluding one meaning or being at odds with another. That's exactly my point. Feng Shui is an interesting example because there, in a poetic way (a strict conceptual framework full of very evocative symbolism), a relationship is established between space, energy and human well-being: "where our language suggests a body, and there is none..." My inter-est in Feng Shui lies just as much in the kinds of issues it addresses as in the way it addresses them.

BART LOOTSMA: It's not so simple that you can solve it with a simple quote. You can't get off unpunished by taking Wittgenstein's work as a plea for religion and superstition. To prove that Wittgenstein recognized the existence of the spiritual (or in his words, the mystical as well), you also could have taken the "Tractatus", but that's completely beside the point. Wittgenstein tried his whole life long to approach the spiritual or to show its presence: in his philosophy, in his sculpture, in his architecture and in his photography. So thus not only in language (and it would have been interesting to see what he would have made of the new media). There are certainly contemporary artists who attempt this as well, like Bill Viola for example. But that's something completely different than using the spiritual as a *means*; Wittgenstein didn't have a recipe for it and I don't think that one exists.

If we're talking about the formation of meaning in the age of technology and capitalism, which of course we're all continuously involved with, I'm more interested in contemporary myths or collectively employed metaphors than in New Age, for example the Bachelor Machine as laid out by Michel Carrouges, or the

NICK WEST: This search for meaning will manage to achieve its goal much more quickly when the two schizophrenic halves of our lives are joined. As long as we live partially in physical space and partially in media space, our attentions will oscillate between the two without coming into any real focus. Part of the solution will lie in breaking down the distinction between media devices and physical space so that there will be a higher degree of integration and seamlessness between the two. But we also need to find some kind of way in which we can think of these two places in the same framework, so that we can design for both of them simultaneously.

Desire Machine as worked out by Deleuze and Guattari. It's a shame that these are both still mechanical metaphors. I'd be curious to see what kinds of myths the media create themselves. Although the myth recalled by the film "Poltergeist" is a variant of an old one, at least it would be something along those lines. I think our belief in numbers also has something of a similar myth within it, certainly if you think of subjectivity: every party is his own expert. Numbers play a crucial role in the contemporary creation of meaning, but in a completely different way than in the Kabbala. Think of the contours around Schiphol Airport, for example. But that would still have to be worked out. "But if you tell them: 'The planet he came from is the asteroid B612', then they'll believe you and they'll let you alone with their questions. They're like that. And you mustn't resent them. Children have to be very patient with grown-ups" -- "The Little Prince", Antoine de Saint-Exupèry.

INFORMATION IN SPACE

DICK RIJKEN: As a fifth point, I'd like to mention information in space: the situated media. Where do we come in contact with information? What information is where, and when is it meaningful? In my car I listen to the radio, in my living room I watch TV, in my workroom I have my PC, I have a buzzer in my pocket, in the train it's the newspaper or a book, etc. There are many implicit connections between different media and different spaces which are often rooted in technology or infrastructure. There's no cable connection on the train, and TVs have only recently become small enough to take along with you. The size of a newspaper or magazine in part determines its place of use, driving a car is an activity which doesn't tolerate any visual media as extra stimuli, etc. Space and timing are now more or less given (at night it's the TV in the living room, all day long in the car it's the radio, etc.), but when, soon, all kinds of objects will be able to wirelessly receive and transmit information, then we can pry apart all of these certainties.

Laptops and, specifically, palmtops are devices we can carry with us, and they can do more and more in terms of multimedia performance. But what does that mean for the information in the devices? The living room is a large social space, the workroom is a small, individual space, my jacket pocket is a very small, personal space. Many interactive appliances are highly individual, and the living room is a pre-eminently social space. What does that mean for the whole idea of interactive television? Will it ever work? Why did CD-i flop, and why is CD-

DICK RIJKEN: The information environments in which media, for example television, appear are becoming different. The television is the "end of the line". The image appears on the TV screen, people watch it, and that's it. Once that same signal is delivered to my computer, it can be the beginning of a new cycle. I can copy and paste images or video sequences and use them in my own documents. I can even publish the results. This has serious consequences for the way content is produced. Information that was designed to be delivered into a social space is not necessarily meaningful in a more private space.

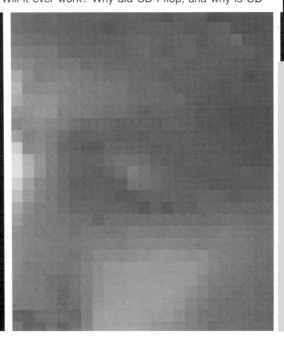

Rom still a growth market? Most PCs are in workrooms, in offices, in extremely individual proximity to the user, whose face is at most a meter away from the monitor. It makes you think of kids who hunch in front of the TV to play a computer game. Can they see it better this way, or are they creating their own personal space?

BART LOOTSMA: All of the small wireless transmitters and receivers will certainly change many certainties within our traditional ideas about, and our experience of, space and position. In fact this has already happened, and we already use all the devices you mentioned in other places both inside and outside of the home. Architects try to facilitate more flexibility in lifestyle by making less unequivocal floor plans, which people can divide as they see fit. And this is not only the result of the new media, by the way; it's also because the traditional family structure is under pressure and the majority of households don't consist of families any more. Sociologists like Beck and Giddens point out that we are now, as opposed to in the industrial society, compelled to design our own biographies, and that is just what we are doing. Precisely for that reason I'm wary about you wanting to know as exactly as possible where certain kinds of information should be offered. Maybe the CD-i flopped because it banked so emphatically

on the traditional position of the TV set. The image of the block of new apartment buildings which all have the TV in the same place is an abhorrence to everyone, isn't it? That some inventions are not immediately catching on now doesn't mean that something similar won't pop up soon that will catch on. Changes in society's organization will perhaps take longer, but that's not to say that the changes won't come. Think of the effects that the arrival of running water on all floors of city apartment buildings had in comparison to the days of the village well, or the effects of plumbing that replaced the mobile sanitation wagon. They're much more significant than simply the installation of a tap and a toilet in the individual apartments. That's exactly why it surprises me that you place so much emphasis on the traditional physical room in which all of the devices have to find their place. That surprised me before as well, when we were discussing the speculations of Nick West about the idea of buildings which broadcast information. It will happen, but I actually find this innovation, in regard to signboards and shop windows for example, to be only marginal. In my view, what's crucial is that these new media and communications networks form spaces themselves which only partially draw something from the physical space. What's more, when they become cordless they mercilessly put pressure on the traditional organization of the physical space, and even replace it. This is

BRUNO FELIX: Since carriers of information are becoming ever smaller, more personal and more mobile, since the available offering of information is becoming ever larger, and the dependence on information ever greater, people will want to use information in more and more places. In architecture, you can see this in the fact that fewer and fewer spaces are being designed exclusively for one intended use; instead they're being designed for multiple uses. People will want to use architecture, or in this sense, space, in more ways, and this will make more and more things possible. Of course the reverse is also true: when people want to use information in more and more places, this has consequences on how information is offered, and on the information itself.

NICK WEST: A useful approach is to compare not the individual actors within each discipline (i.e. designers) but instead to compare the social and cultural effects of the overall system produced by the two disciplines. From this direction, the convergence of the two disciplines points to a merger of cyberspace and real space into a metaspace, or simply a living space, that includes elements of both. This convergence is coming from both directions: real space is becoming more ephemeral as our connection to specific geographic places diminishes, and our attention becomes more focused on our presence in cyberspace through mobile phones, computer communication, and ubiquitous media of all types. And cyberspace is becoming more immanent and permanent, like the real spaces that we have already become familiar with. With e-mail addresses and the spread of personal "handles" for ICQ or other chat and messaging systems, we are becoming enmeshed in an architecture of identity - a "place" where we can always be contacted. Merging these two trends creates the possibility of an integrated hierarchy of spaces, with virtual spaces existing that are both connected to and unconnected from the current hierarchy of spaces we

inhabit. In a sense, this is the 21st century version of the urban planner's street grid - the overlaying of a virtual, abstract layer on top of an already existing reality. The introduction of these new, virtual layers on top of the existing city could be a powerful democratizing force in the current power structures of urban space. The city in this future model becomes a palimpsest of malleable, virtual overlays: always shifting, and yet retaining persistence. Think of it as an interactive, city-wide, and sophisticated version of the layers of posters and announcements that accumulate on kiosks or lamp-posts. In this model, the barrier of entry for potential urban authors is much lower than in the current concrete-and-steel cities we inhabit. Like the initial burst of do-it-yourself publishing efforts that occurred on the Internet when it first became widely available, the introduction of this capability to annotate the physical city could produce a similar explosion of urban revisions. The random city collages of the Situationists, once perceptible only through writing and conversation, can now be painted on top of the physical city for anyone to see, at any time.

already happening, and it extends beyond a virus that changes genetic materi-al: it's the Invasion of the Bodysnatchers. It's interesting that you mention, among the living room and the study with their seemingly secure walls, also the car and the train (and why not by airplane, by the way?). After all, we no longer live only in the neighbourhood or in the city: we also live within global mobility and communications networks. We even have addresses for these places when we're on the road. The most remarkable thing about all this is how normal it's already become over a short period of time. A student of mine at the Berlage Instituut, Peter Trummer, came up with a nice term for it. He rightly proposes that what's involved is no longer the place, but rather the "polygamy of the place". When we use the phone, listen to the radio, watch TV, play computer games or use the Internet, of course we're in a specific place. But what's much more important at that moment is that we're in contact with another place. That's why we do it, and thus the other place is in a certain sense more important than the first. Yet what's crucial is the fusion of the two; this is our most intense longing. We all long so strongly for polygamy that conjugal jealousy hardly counts any more. The living room is only such a small social place. The devices you men-tion give access to an impossibly large amount of much more interesting social spaces. We need to completely rethink living in the polygamous place. The

physical space inside it becomes a space time, a space in which the nearness is more determined by the time required to bridge the distance than by the phys-ical distance. Since its beginnings, the development of the media has gone hand in hand with the development of mobility. Consider postal traffic and the stage-coach, the train and the telegraph, the airplane and the radio, and the spaceship and satellite traffic. Yet it's about more than just the historical relationship between the development of the various networks as infrastructure in and of itself. Media and mobility act as catalysts for each other. We not only spend less and less time at home due to our everyday concerns or our use of free time, but we also travel more over long distances and move house increasingly frequent-ly. Leaving out this step in the considerations on media and architecture is an insurmountable obstacle. So if we look at the mobility and media networks, regardless of the device that arranges the accessibility, the sphere of influence of the specific device and its attendant network is probably more important than the physical and geographical set of borders: clothes, room, building, district, city, province, country. Then we're dealing with the audibility of the sound, for example, or the visibility of the image, combined with the reach of the network. With this last point, I'm getting at the effect that we all know when we're driving along, listening to the car radio, and then we drive beyond the reach of the radio

BART LOOTSMA: Working late one night, I had a ghostly experience. I heard strange noises from the garbage can in our kitchen. They appeared to be fragments of conversa-tions on the police radio. When I opened the lid, the voices disappeared. When I closed it again, they slowly came back. At first I thought my neighbor downstairs, a district attorney, was following a police action he was involved in. But when I asked him the next day, of course he laughed at me, suggesting that I had been watching too much televi-sion - which he in turn can hear from his bed. Months later it appeared that it was my other neighbor from next door, a lonely divorced housewife. Ever since she had to evacuate her house one night because the house next to it was on fire, she's been turning on the scanner at night, listening to the police frequencies. She sleeps lightly, but whenever the name of the street we live on is mentioned, she is immedi-ately alert and puts on her clothes, waiting to be rescued. The dustbin in my kitchen must have worked as a kind of amplifier, very much like when you put a glass on the wall to be able to hear what people are talking about in the next room. What is the point of these observations? I think it's the paradoxical experience of both isolation, intimacy (the

individual alone in his or her room, while everyone is asleep, in a house surrounded by a vast darkness) and the aware-ness of the continuous presence of "them", of "the others", far - or less far - away, trying to make contact, desperately trying to unveil their identity, to get in touch. It is a slum-bering awareness, but one that we all share. Every one of us knows the experience of jumping up when a telephone rings, even if it is in another room, in another house or on television. And the disbelief and disappointment if it is not for you. To make sure anyone can get in touch with us any-time, we carry cell phones and beepers. The radio and the television function as media, as kinds of crystal balls. The scanner is the institutionalized form of this. But "they" are here, or at least "they" must be there: "This program has been recorded in front of a live studio audience". If they hadn't said that, one would doubt whether it had really hap-pened. The studio audience functions as a witness for the public at home. The police are the official, institutionalized witnesses who make it so attractive to listen to a scanner. (extract from unpublished manuscript "The New Land-scape")

BERT MULDER: Consider how people use the telephone, for example. The phone used to hang in the hallway, and it was at a height which allowed only your father to make calls. And when it rang, it was so loud that everyone in the house would wake up immediately. Over the past fifty years, the telephone has become smaller and smaller, has been freed from the wall, and been moved to the living room. People began to have two telephones, and the phones became portable. The fact that phones became cordless resulted in people beginning to use them differently. You also see a similar development with the television set. It used to be a large, complicated and expensive device which led people to arrange their whole living rooms around it, a bit like an open fireplace without a fire. At night, the television was turned on and people would sit themselves down on the sofa with a cup of coffee to watch the evening news on the Netherlands' Channel 1. You now see two developments. On one hand, people are buying very small TVs, which they turn on very quickly just to catch the news. And at the same time, people are buying mammoth, large-screen televisions with insane sound systems, and then once again arranging their whole houses around them. The television becomes

station. It's more than a technical problem, because it has cultural consequences. On a small scale, this comes up in Nick West's proposal for speaking buildings. Jean Francois Lyotard also made use of this in the "Les Immateriaux" exhibition, where every artwork defined an interior space by means of a small transmitter, which also determined the actual space of the exhibition architecture. On a larger scale, we recognize this from the radio stations in Los Angeles, all of which have their own individual signatures. And on a global scale, the borders appear in the form of the language that's used on the Internet, for example, and the degree of censorship. Sometimes the borders of certain media's spheres of influence correspond to physical, legal and geographical borders, but far from always. We know this from the commercial radio and television broadcasters in the Netherlands who began outside of our national borders, for example. That the new media networks are increasingly replacing the frameworks of traditional architecture and urban planning is evinced by phenomena such as electric arrest. And in Tokyo there's now even a mobile phone for children to buy: the Doraemon, designed in light blue with a pink outline, equipped with technology that allows parents to establish exactly where their child is in the city. They then call the central telephone network and get sent a fax with a map.

DICK RIJKEN: I completely agree with you about the historical connection between communication and mobility. Napoleon supplied France with an infrastructure of roads because he wanted to transform "farmers" into "French citizens". Of course we're now living in networks of meaning which are grounded in media and communications technology. You're overlooking the cultural dimension of media tied to a particular area if you compare these media with signboards. The difference lies precisely in their multiplicity, and, hand in hand with that, freedom. The signboard is what it is. One person can interpret it differently than someone else, but that's where it ends. With digital media, the singular place can open up an entire spectrum of information. I then have access to an entire collection of perspectives on the place. And then who will I allow to tell me the place's story? If you want something to compare it with, a better example is the tourist guide: the one published by the Dutch Touring Club gives a different perspective than the "Rough Guide". But I can decide for myself which one I take with me. Or I can take them both, or neither; it's my choice.

CHRISTOPHER ALEXANDER

DICK RIJKEN: Thinking from the perspective of situations and experience is the

an entertainment center that gives you a kind of home-cinema experience. When you live in a row house and you install a Bose surround sound system, you have serious problems if you don't have the same taste as your neighbors do. So if you're someone who consumes a lot of media, you either have to go live on a farm or do something about your walls. The television is now a device that you turn on for a bit of diversion, but you don't use it for your household chores. And computers are mainly used by kids for playing games, and by working people who use them for word processing. So people sit at the computer all by themselves, usually in the study or in a separate corner of the living room. When the television and the computer converge in one machine, it will become much more of a consumer medium, a medium people will use to communicate, to buy things and to receive services. Computers will see to it that people will begin to do things more actively; they won't passively sit in front of the TV as often. With the Internet, you get an information network in your own living room, where for example your community, your insurance company, the Red Cross and your friends are all present at the same time. You get a much different feeling with this

kind of device, because it becomes something you use to keep in contact with other people.

NICK WEST: There's also now the Lovegety, a personal beeper with settings for "karaoke", "chat" and "friends". If you get within 15 meters of someone with their beeper on the same setting, they both go off! Suddenly faceless crowds can become differentiated by your personal preference.

BART LOOTSMA: The different GPS navigation systems that are currently being developed for use in cars give a perfect idea about the merging of media and architecture on the level of urbanism. Last year in Berlin I took a ride in a taxi that was equipped with a test version of just such a system by Siemens. The taxi driver, a sixty-five year old man who was obviously an electronics freak, typed in the destination and was guided there by a voice that told him not only when to turn left or right, but even gave him advice about what lane to choose.

BERT MULDER: If you want to create an environment that is fully flexible, that continuously adapts to the change that represents the context, where nothing is fixed, where we only have flows, where we only have change, what you wind up doing is creating a generic infrastructure. An infrastructure that can be continuously adaptive all the time, and that can be controlled from a distance. The way we survive at the end of the 20th century is by "global remote control". That's what Western thinking gave to the world. Western thinking focused its attention on the material side of things, and so what we actually spread over the world are global infrastructures that sustain material production. There's a global infrastructure for money, for design, for logistics, for the handling of materials, for production. That's what sustains the world at the moment, and that's what we did. We, meaning Western scientific thinking. That's our contribution to the world. By standardization, by the fact that I can remotely control them, these structures allow for immense variation. The interesting thing is that people think standardization leads to uniformity, while the opposite is true. There's an explosion in design, an explosion in variation based on standardization.

reason why many interaction designers are so charmed by architect Christopher Alexander (specifically "the timeless way of building" and "a pattern language"). After his flirtation with formal specifications in "Notes on the Synthesis of Form", Alexander has turned 180 degrees and now tries in "pattern language" to give a structure to the issues in design without impairing direct experience or otherwise formulating rigid laws. What's interesting is that in all his "patterns", he also very explicitly involves context in his design advice: all design is situated. Someone please tell me why every architect gets sick if they even hear the name Alexander...

BART LOOTSMA: It seems to me that thinking about situations and experience from Alexander's perspective is only worthwhile for firms which want to develop products for the short-term, as a kind of market research. And we know that market researchers now, as always, have to proceed from the standpoint of the existing situation, and that they don't have time to consider things any further than their noses are long. During the Masterclass, Greg Lynn joked that media designers might value Alexander because they themselves aren't people, but cyborgs. There's a germ of wisdom in that if we think about robots who, once they've been activated and furnished with a secret message, first want to adapt themselves as much as possible to their new environment by means of a learning process so that their true objective doesn't become conspicuous. As we know, this always misfires because they take what they learn too literally and aren't able to cope with new situations, situations they often create themselves. "A Pattern Language" is a terribly thick book which I very reluctantly had to read sections of twenty years ago. At this point I can't really steep myself in it in any detail. It might well be the case that a rereading would turn up some new things, but this would surprise me, as the people who appreciated the book back then were extremely conservative, and they didn't tolerate any kind of innovation or deviation. Architect Tom Frantzen, who not so long ago distilled a number of new patterns himself from the current situation during his study at the Technical University in Eindhoven (a practice which Alexander encourages in his book) pointblank got an "F" for it. One of the patterns he proposes even contains "398: The TV". I think that the biggest problem with "A Pattern Language" is that Alexander distilled his patterns from the commissions he was personally involved with during the period of eight years which preceded the publication of his book in 1977. He then elevates them to a language which makes a claim to general applicability and timelessness. And all of this despite the question of whether architecture and urban planning, as he describes them, are indeed a

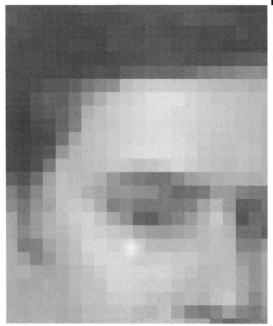

language which precedes life, as Alexander suggests. Of course a language allows neologisms, but I think the difference is much more essential. Architecture and urban planning follow life; they react to it, and not the other way around. This fact is only obscured by the fact that old buildings and existing cities can often be adapted to new functions and meanings. But that's more a question of typology than of language. There are legions of Alexander's contemporaries who developed more interesting ideas for media designers in the sixties and seventies, since mobility and media play a prominent role here. I'm thinking for example of Archigram, Superstudio, Archizoom, Coop Himmelblau, Haus Rucker Co, Hans Hollein, Paul Virilio, our own Constant, and many others. It's no accident that now, after the regressive fracture of the seventies and eighties in which the belief and thereby the interest in technology had all but completely disappeared, there is once again an unbelievable amount of interest in their work and hardly any in Alexander.

DICK RIJKEN: First of all, in my view this all has more to do with Alexander's methodology than with his results: the way he analyzes human activities is considered by many of my colleagues to be very inspiring. Furthermore, it's becoming increasingly clear to me that many of our differences of opinion revolve

around context-dependent design. Media designers seem to accept this easily, while architects abhor it. You guys have noticed over time that buildings have to accommodate new functions again and again, but this is much less the case with us. There'll be another newspaper tomorrow, and a new edition of a magazine next month. We already discussed this before, but this also touches upon our discussion about infrastructure.

Both buildings as well as websites structure people's actions and can therefore be seen as infrastructure. And both are also implements, cultural products. I sense an emphasis in many of your remarks on the infrastructural aspect of architecture. It not only has to do with the structuring of users' actions; architecture is also, as in the examples of Koolhaas, becoming an infrastructure for media. But of course context-dependence is a difficult concept in relation to infrastructure. It's much more relevant if we're talking about specific examples. Thus we can compare the Internet to standards and protocols in the building industry, and compare websites to buildings. I think the key to why media does want to work in a context-dependent way, and architecture does not, lies in tempo and speed. We can make a new newspaper every day and update a website, and do all of this for target groups which are becoming increasingly small. That makes it at once possible and necessary for us to work in an ever more

GREG LYNN: Christopher Alexander is a somewhat forgotten but still provocative theorist, and many contemporary architects have incorporated many of his strategies and concepts, for example the New Urbanists. But as a model for design, his work is universally dismissed by architects. The worst thing that ever happened to Christopher Alexander is that he started being perceived as an architect rather than as an architectural theorist.

BERT MULDER: When you look at the main distinction between media and architecture, architecture's border is determined from the outside. In media, this border is continuously re-created by my mind, it is a re-created order. You can actually tie together the external form and the internal experience which is continuously being re-created, and then organize it in practice. We actually converge on event spaces. For me, Christopher Alexander's pattern language is a series of event spaces. The remarks on Christopher Alexander remind me of a possible difference between media and architecture. Where architecture searches for inspiration by breaking the mold into a dynamic flow of creation, media and information designers seek to

order the existing dynamic of increasing information. One creates meaning through the destruction of the existing, while the other creates meaning through the construction of the existing. I didn't see Alexander's work as a language prescribing what to build, but rather as a language describing what happens when you let people make their own things. As a careful inventory of life creating "anonymous history", rather than as a stark set of patterns for those without imagination.

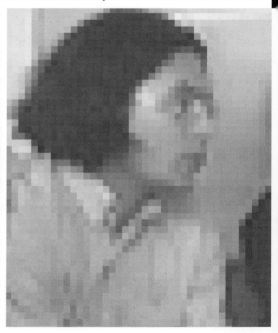

context-dependent way. What kind of information can the VPRO offer on small hand-held computers, for example? And when? Where and when is information about films most relevant? In the living room? On the street in front of the cinema? In the video shop? The designing of media is becoming more and more situated. I was talking before about the consumer as part of the result; here we see the same thing happening. If I know where a user is, then space becomes an integral part of the result. How do architects consider the location of information within a space?

BART LOOTSMA: As you might infer from my above comments, in a much broader way then you propose. I think that architects hope that information will become available everywhere. In principle it is that way already.

INFRASTRUCTURE

DICK RIJKEN: We're once again in the midst of the discussion about infrastructure: generic media infrastructures which come in contact with generic spatial infrastructures and enter into an interaction. But what criteria do these kinds of infrastructures need to fulfill in order to enable the interaction?

BART LOOTSMA: Wirelessness would be very nice.

DICK RIJKEN: I mean more along the lines of our earlier remarks about meaning and the formation of meaning. Like you said, "the architectural space isn't just a bearer of meaning itself, but it helps facilitate the generation of the meanings which are determined within it. And perhaps it excludes one meaning, or is at odds with another one." Try replacing "architecture" with "infrastructure" and then think of infrastructures that facilitate context-dependence... What statements could we then make about the qualities of infrastructures like these?

BART LOOTSMA: I do indeed think that this is a similar discussion. It depends quite a lot on the infrastructure's objective. Don't be too particular, I would say.

DICK RIJKEN: For us, openness is a crucial characteristic of information environments. The WWW exists by the grace of a generic, open standard which everyone can make use of. If we develop systems for internal communication, then the environments have to be able to encompass many kinds of information. Take the 24-hour Cinema Service for example once again. The user interface is based on an open structure that works with "filters": with a filter, a selection can

LARS SPUYBROEK: People always seem to think that information is something like language or coding, like a text or an image that one puts on a wall. To architects, information is more like a complex of forces that make up form, and the structure of it informs action. That's why we shouldn't distinguish too severely between infrastructure and event, thinking that this infrastructure, in its striving for the generic, could become the greatest common denominator of all possible actions and thus become neutral and absent. It's a classic illusion in architecture that when one designs for all possibilities, so that "everything can happen", actually nothing happens, because this structure does not view itself as an event as well, but rather only as a hall or shell. There is interaction only when the structure/form is an act in itself, not a specific act, nor a generic one, but a multiplication of action. In getting away form the standard plan and program (one act in one place, named function), media could help and should saturate architecture, not only technically but also conceptually. Buildings should not be a formal reduction of action, a low resolution of standardized and disciplined behavior; indeed, they should instead be responsive, but not "smart", and develop reactive patterning not to comfort or pacify situations, but instead to engage and "enactivate".

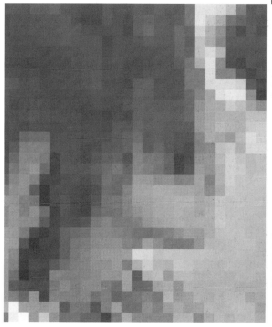

be made from the large database (for example, by using the "genre" filter to select only "thrillers"). We've made it in such a way that we can very easily add new filters or get rid of old ones. The underlying structure is very generic. And yet the Cinema Service was very much designed from an unambiguous vision regarding people, users and situations of use. The underlying assumption is that the VPRO wants to give its audience tools for finding their way through the enormous net of information we find ourselves in. But this tool indeed bears a VPRO signature: information from the Dutch film magazine SKRIEN and from the Rotterdam Film Festival, but not from the "de Telegraaf" tabloid or the film guide PREVIEW. You now find the signature primarily in the sort of information that's in the system, but it expands to the tools within the system as well, for example a VPRO filter which users can employ to keep up on films on TV that are recommended by the VPRO. But it won't be so paternalistic that we'll exclude films from our system that we consider to be bad, or that we won't keep you informed of films made by directors who are third-rate in our eyes. By making the information architecture layered (a generic, slowly changing lower layer and a specific, flexible upper layer), we're trying to be strategic and up-to-date at the same time. Infrastructure for context-dependency. How do architects deal with issues like these?

BART LOOTSMA: I think this is analogous to the traditional distinctions and connections between urban planning and architecture, or architecture and interior design.

INFORMATION AGAINST SPACE

DICK RIJKEN: As the penultimate relationship between space and information, we have information against space: the Global Village. At some point, communications technology levels out cultures and ideas which are bound to a specific place. We all watch CNN and drink Coca Cola, and the Gulf War took place primarily in the media. Is an urbanite urban because he lives in the city, or because he has an urban worldview? It seems physical location is becoming an ever smaller factor in determining our ideas. What does this actually mean for the designing of districts in villages or cities? How has architecture reacted to these issues up until now?

BART LOOTSMA: That's a bit too vast for architecture. But that's not to say that if architects don't deal with this issue, recognizable and ordered processes of urbanization won't appear. A good friend of mine, one of the most talented

LARS SPUYBROEK: Obviously the Global Village, or the Omnipolis, as Virilio calls it, has meant the steady deterioration of the landscape, the horizon and the "public sphere" (which is also a machine constructed by perspective, just like the Renaissance, the old wooden scaffolding of axes and squares). Now the atomization continues precisely because of the hyper-global structuring of events by media. So we'll get more and more vacuum-sealed villages and entities like shopping malls, virtual or gated communities floating in nothingness, or asphalt lakes, because the structure of light that was first supplied by the architecture of the polis (police and politics) has now been taken over by media (others would say augmented). So now, when an event happens somewhere, anywhere, it is no longer figured against the urban ground, nor is it a face against the landscape. There are now only faces, faces imploding into faces, there is only transmission of interiors and intimacy, without facades in-between them. Just look at a talk show or at Stelarc or Steve Mann. Much like we lived in the face of Diana for a while. Architecture should not react by either retreating into tectonics or fleeing into bigness; it should make these concepts its own, and restructure or transform them.

designers of my generation who went back to the countryside of Zeeland to grow his own vegetables after completing his studies, once complained to me in his typical dialect about the fact that the farmers in his area had also become city people; they listened to expensive stereos in their air-conditioned tractors and were just as reachable with their mobile phones as everyone else was. According to him, their urbanity manifested itself not only in the fact that they could be contacted, but also in the fact that they had adopted a different pattern of consumption. A tractor wasn't replaced when it could no longer plow anymore, but when it had became unfashionable. The farmers now only go for an evening out when they go to the big city. Western farmers are, in terms of globalization, perhaps the most developed people of all. They constantly keep abreast of international stock quotations and markets because the majority of what they produce is exported. They really know everything about El Niño. Their companies are connected to every international transportation and communications network possible. The French wine-grower, who we know in the world of architecture from his beautiful Herzog & de Meuron designed farm in the Napa Valley near San Francisco, also has vineyards in France.

In Australia, we find the best example of new urbanization patterns which are influenced by new communications media and mobility. Two students of mine at the Berlage Institute Amsterdam, Penelope Dean and Peter Trummer, are currently doing exceptionally interesting research into this. Although there were predecessors to the Flying Doctors who made use of mission stations, railways and telegraphs, it all really got going only with the introduction of an open radio system and the use of the first airplanes at the end of the twenties. A structure, based on the reach of airplanes and radio transmitters, now covers almost the entire continent. The Flying Doctors not only brought about the airline Quantas, but the open radio system is also used for educational goals and for the members to communicate with one another. All in all, the Flying Doctors enabled an exceptionally spare pattern of urbanization in which the inhabitants, when speaking with each other via the radio systems, use a language which sociolinguists characterize as "urban". People who live hundreds of kilometers away from each other consider themselves, interestingly enough, "neighbors". I think that the same phenomenon as this Australian one would also be perceptible in other places if it weren't for the fact that the physical presence of traditional patterns of urbanization obscures their view.

But perhaps there are even more radical perspectives on the horizon. Right now, there is a flood of cruise ships being built. This is due to the fact that a large share of their "cabins" are being built as time-share apartments, just like on Ibiza

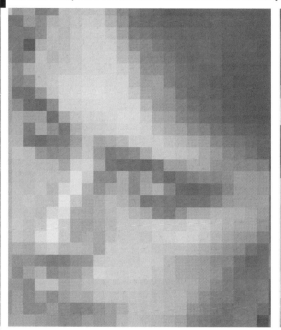  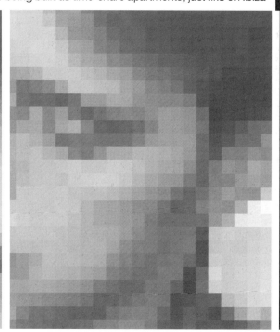

and all the other vacation islands. Thus the cruise ship is actually becoming a sailing vacation village, a small city, which is somewhere else on the planet every time you visit. Using the media, you can find out where it is and then fly there. Perhaps Archigram's concept for the Walking City wasn't so far-fetched after all. I could imagine that multinationals would be interested in sailing offices like these; they could have everything on board for their employees, and the ship could simply dock at the site that was the most economically attractive at that moment. In fact, one of Bill Gates' partners has such a ship under construction right now.

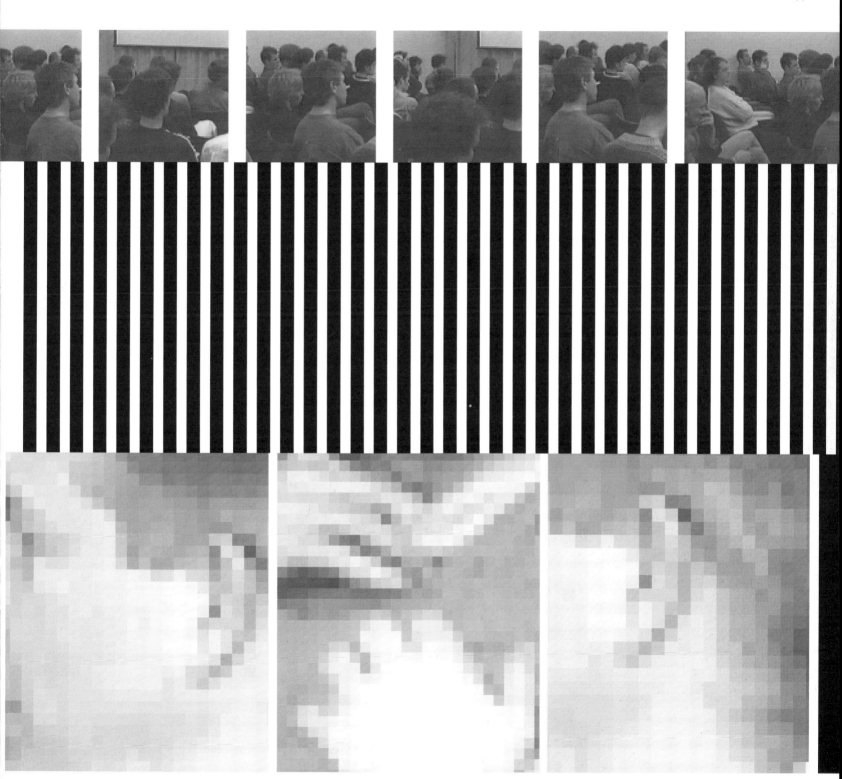

BERT MULDER: WE THINK IN TERMS OF OBJECTS AND NOT IN TERMS IN FLOWS, WE THINK IN THINGS, MORE THAN IN PROCESSES

NICK WEST: THE ADDITION OF LAYERS OF "VIRTUAL" ARCHITECTURE COULD LEAD TO A NEW CONCEPTION OF CITIES AS COLLECTIONS OF INFORMATIC FLOWS

BART LOOTSMA: MEDIA CREATE INDEPENDENT SPACES IN A WAY THAT ARCHITECTURE WOULD NEVER BE ABLE TO DO

GREG LYNN: ARCHITECTS WORK AS A NETWORK OF EXPERTISE, BUT THEY HAVE YET TO INCLUDE MEDIA

WINY MAAS: WHEN YOU SEE MEDIA AS A WORLD OF POSSIBLE MEETINGS, VIRTUAL OR REAL, THIS MIGHT GIVE ARCHITECTURE A MODEL OF RETHINKING PUBLIC SPACES

DICK RIJKEN: THERE'S MORE TO IT THAN MEETS THE EYE THROUGH WEIRD SPECTACLES THAT MAKE YOU LOOK LIKE ROBOCOP....

MEDIA AND ARCHITECTURE

DICK RIJKEN: Finally the question: where do architecture and media come in contact? It has now become clear that it's getting harder and harder for media designers to make information systems without considering the spatial contexts in which the information will wind up, and that we therefore have to make contact with architects and urban planners. But during the Masterclass I noticed there were quite a few misunderstandings because people were speaking from different lines of approach. On the other hand, I see an important role being reserved for media and information technology in facilitating the way that complex building projects are realized: communicating with the involved parties, editing the content for a complex project and carefully offering it to the relevant people, facilitating discussions with stake-holders, visualizing and simulating future situations, etc. This refers to your remarks on SimCity and similar tools.

TOOLS

DICK RIJKEN: In my opinion, we can introduce interfaces between a number of areas: first of all, the tools we use. We use computers with Photoshop, drawings, diagrams, etc. You all do, too. Can I allow a public inquiry commission to experience how the new road would transform their route from home to work?

BART LOOTSMA: Absolutely, there's already vehement experimentation going on in this area. Furthermore, the use of the same tools simplifies the exchange of files. But immediately, I think that's as far as it goes. This sort of tool is the standard material of every designer, regardless of the field.

TECHNIQUES AND NOTATION

DICK RIJKEN: Secondly, techniques and notation. We work a lot with prototypes and partial products which are undergoing testing. For us it's fairly easy to quickly make a working prototype as a "proof of concept". We often represent information spaces in the form of flowcharts, tree diagrams and network diagrams, and sometimes (paper) story-boards with displays to illustrate the possible walkthroughs. Often a test is conducted with users at several points in the process to see if what is expected to happen actually does. But we don't have any standard way of modeling or representing the "space of use", and then I'm not even getting into spatial dynamics...

BART LOOTSMA: I think the flowcharts, tree diagrams and network diagrams have been developed in architecture based on the analogy of industry (Taylor,

WINY MAAS: I think the exhibition world is one of the places where the disciplines are totally merging together. Even big exhibitions are now being set up in this way, because you already partly experience them in your office or at home. And when you go there physically because you want to meet people, those people are sometimes represented in other media like films, brochures or advertisements. So this occasions yet another kind of exhibition space. Furthermore, you see children nowadays growing up with all kinds of media. Education is changing as well, and will definitely change the concept of the building and the house in the end. So architecture and media are merging.

MICHAEL HENSEL: Media initially effects architecture in a two-fold way, first of all by enabling media technology. Advanced telecommunication and computational technology enable the integration of several contingent groups of participants into the design process from the very beginning, via direct access to the project's dataset. Through access being continuously available in the making of the project, designers, clients and specialized consultants can all simultaneously partake in the design process and can

drive the project towards a complex and advanced resolution issued by inclusive and continuous datasets. The new technologies facilitate a flexible system with a high capacity for absorbing and benefiting from multiplicituous input and data exchange. Secondly, you see the influence of media in generative media technology. New computational technology, as a generative tool, offers a range of new design techniques that allow for the production of new spatial organization and articulation. The possibility of involving large quantities of variables allows for the derivation of more complex spatial configurations and dissolves the necessity of prioritizing any particular phase in the design process. This means the diminishing of inconsistencies between the virtual modeling of space on one hand, and the manufacturing of the actual space on the other, i.e. via rapid prototyping and the establishment of continuous datasets. Eventually, digital processing will be able to free manufacturing from the constraints of modular production. Modulated variability: the chance to manufacture continuous difference instead of continuous sameness.

BERT MULDER: Architects and media designers are using the same tools more and more often. The architecture students in this Masterclass all use the same six software packages as the media students do. But the fact that they use each other's language or tools doesn't detract from the fact that there are significant differences in their working methods.

GREG LYNN: There's a convergence of expertise in hardware and software. A lot of jobs are defined by software skills, and that's why architects can work in media. We asked the students in the Masterclass which software they used, and they all use the six same packages.

Ford). This doesn't detract from the fact that the representation of the "space of use", as you call it, is the most difficult thing there is. At most, architects work with data gathered from experience, thousands of examples of which are recorded in the famous handbook by Neufert, for example. Establishing the minimum measurements necessary for a specific function is still the easiest thing to do. In the twenties and thirties there was a lot of research done into this (the "Wohnung für das Existenzminimum" ("Apartment for a minimal income") was an important theme at the CIAM), and in the fifties as well. Now it is primarily specialized firms involved in projects who draw up expanded programs for the client, programs which detail the various requirements and the attendant number of square meters needed, and the architect then has to comply with these requirements during the design. There are still quite a few norms and regulations, like for example those established in the Occupational Health and Safety legislation. The responsibility for the program is thus only partially in the architect's hands.

If we want to consider this more broadly, then there have been a number of attempts made throughout history to get a better grip on the "space of use". The problem, after all, is that people don't only use a space in the way it was directly developed for, as the functionalists thought; instead, people (luckily) demonstrate all kinds of other unpredictable behavior. Once again it was Bernard Tschumi who did a lot of research into this; he tried to apply notational techniques from dance (choreography), the military, sports (tactics), music and film. The easiest thing to get a grip on, relatively, is large numbers of users and streams of people, of cars, or of whatever else. These are also areas in which the computer is suddenly enabling a breakthrough, as this data is readily manageable in all kinds of animation programs based on topological mathematics, programs used for example by Greg Lynn, Ben van Berkel, and now NOX as well. These programs also lend themselves well to study the spatial dynamics of a design.

If we're really talking about spatial dynamics, for example the growth of a city, then I have high expectations of programs which are based on artificial life. Prototypes are only rarely used in architecture because of the high costs, though sometimes test models of (parts of) buildings are made on a scale of 1:1. Here as well I expect a lot from the development of computer technology because with it, better simulations of processes can be made.

DICK RIJKEN: With media as an integral component of the processes...

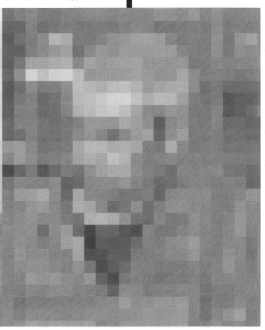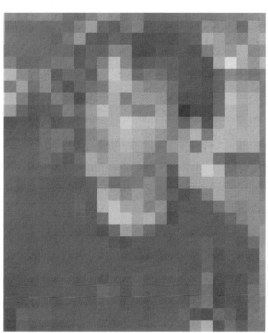

 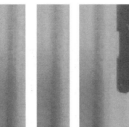     

METHODOLOGY

DICK RIJKEN: The third point in the collaboration between architecture and media is the methodology. As mentioned before, we work very cyclically: analysis, design, test, research, design, etc. Sometimes it's not clear when a design is done because we always keep on tinkering with it. This touches upon our previous remarks on evolutionary design ("too bad, better luck next time"). Does this impede collaboration?

BART LOOTSMA: It's hard for me to judge that. Certainly the tempo of the construction process is increased in such a way that architects can react sooner to the results of their previous work. And of course architects are also constantly tinkering with their work.

LANGUAGE

DICK RIJKEN: The fourth point is language. Media and architecture speak totally different languages; this is specifically made clear when we use the same words and yet actually mean completely different things or associations by them. What is space? What is infrastructure? What is a system? What is a user? What is meaning? I think it would be quite interesting to investigate the patterns of thinking used in our fields a bit more deeply. We find a good example of how media and architecture might be able to arrive at a common language in the "event space" concept that Bert Mulder and Lars Spuybroek used during the Masterclass: an event space is defined in terms of potential effects, and can be realized by means of information, space or both. For example, let's say I want to keep you from coming into my garden. I can build a wall (architecture) or employ a "no trespassing" sign and a police officer (information). Thus we can define the event spaces first, and then afterwards consider what we can design physically and in terms of information.

BART LOOTSMA: Exactly. But the most interesting thing about Lars' approach is that he completely integrates a given concept so that the distinction between architecture and media no longer exists.

MENTALITY

DICK RIJKEN: And finally, the mentality which the designer adopts. I got the

GREG LYNN: When we started this seminar, we asked the architects if they knew any media theorists or whether they had a favorite graphic designer. They couldn't name one. So architects know nothing about the history, theory or practice of media. The media students, on the other hand, all knew several architects and even had favorites. One thing that has to happen is that architects need to understand that, just as they use a structural or mechanical engineer, they need to build teams that include media designers. Architects work as a kind of network of expertise, but they have yet to include media. Architects have to be a bit more intelligent and strategic about how to enter into a dialogue with media. Otherwise they just get used for their skills. Personally, working with media designers made me realize that media has to communicate messages, whereas in architecture it's no longer a priority to represent. Media does have to represent in a very strong way, and therefore a lot of decisions are based on communication. In architecture, communication is something that is almost hardwired in the people: space doesn't have to communicate directly, only at a very basic organizational level. That notion makes me think of architecture differently.

BERT MULDER: I think collaboration between the media world and architecture is very exciting, because a new language is being developed. When you make a new building, you have to begin to totally rethink where media and architecture will converge. A new building has an effect on how the VPRO works, and thus the question becomes how you make a building which will allow the VPRO to remain a good and solid broadcasting organization, both now and ten years from now. For example, if you consider what a broadcasting organization actually is, then you see that it doesn't consist solely of television programs. The VPRO consists of an infrastructure of buildings, program makers, and target groups; it's a network of various sorts of information such as text, sound and video. A VPRO product has to be made from all of these parts. You have to strive for a building which facilitates certain events and which best allows the broadcaster's objectives to be realized. You no longer opt for a new office, a tree house, or thirteen villas, but instead you design a VPRO architecture, an architecture that encompasses both the organization of people, activities and buildings as well as the broadcaster's money flow or the format of the VPRO magazine. And an architec-

ture like this has to optimally support the VPRO's work and ideas. I think it's important to develop the kind of infrastructure where media and architecture come together from one philosophical idea. During the Masterclass, we tried to find just such a common language for media and architecture. If we talk about architecture and about the integration of architecture and media, we're actually talking about the integration of the design of spatial structures and the design of mental structures. The entirety of information technology is our way of dealing with the increasing complexity. All of the mega-trends, all of the mega-developments, and all of the mega-industries are really the human way of dealing with this restructuring of complexity. In this Masterclass, you can see on a small scale that the languages which deal with the different sciences are incapable of talking with each other. It's mainly a problem of language, of getting there, of design methodology. We think in terms of objects and not in terms in flows, we think in things, more than in processes.

LARS SPUYBROEK: During the Masterclass, we (both students and masters) came up with concepts like "beach-

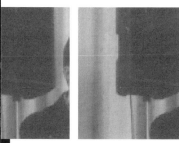

impression during the Masterclass that there were major differences on this point amongst the participants. I think that many differences of opinion can be traced back to the conflict between the artist and the designer, the conflict between autonomy and servitude. You also see this within the media world itself: from "I make what I want to make" to "give the public what they want". At the moment there's an active discussion going on within art education about the fate of the autonomous artist. The entire concept of "autonomy" presupposes non-servitude; in an information society that pushes key concepts like "context" and "relationship", this is a difficult starting position. But it's such an enticing ambition for eager egos... is the autonomous artist a typically twentieth century phenomenon?

BART LOOTSMA: It's definitely time that this matter be discussed within art education. The autonomous artist is indeed a typically twentieth century phenomenon and was given a powerful boost in the post-war period: on one hand, due to the importance that was attached to the individual after the liberation, and on the other hand from the perspective of the Art Sacré, the church which wanted to use modern art to give faith a new aura. Of course divine inspiration played an important role in this last concept, and the artist became an especially impor-

tant person. The visual arts distanced themselves from this position in the sixties, firstly with performance art, and then later with installations in which architecture played an important role. Both visual artists as well as critics demonstrated that the artist had long not been as autonomous as he would have liked to present himself. At the Dutch art academies, where the "autonomous artist" was protected, nourished and cuddled for decades, this has led to an appalling idleness, laziness and superficiality which emanates to other fields. This in turn leads to architects easily being able to write off the innovative work of colleagues as "art", while there are many visual artists for whom architecture might provide the necessary boost, because they can much more easily deal with new situations and develop cultural concepts for them.

INFLUENCE

BART LOOTSMA: Architecture, urban planning and media influence one another in many different ways, and I think they're becoming more and more connected. It seems as if they might even become totally merged in the future. This leads to different kinds of questions from the architectural perspective imposing themselves on the mentality of architecture and the organization of physical space.

ness" and "dinnerness". And everything charging these events/situations was of the same importance - no foreground, no background: the faces, the bodies, the voices and noises, the fabric, the food, the rhythm, the colors, the textile, the sand (the intelligence of the sand: hard when wet, it is a highway, while soft when dry, it is a bed). The essence was that it all became one synthetic image, not an analytical construction - because it was the "tectonics of the image" that were actually best at describing the meta-level of a notion such as "beachness". So, luckily not one of the students came up with the things that keep on slowing down this discussion, no "electronic wallpaper", no Ito-esque Modernism of architecture carrying (and disappearing in) media. On one hand, architecture students drew dynamic, almost meteorological maps of event spaces and used them to create architecture. On the other hand, interaction designers came up with (infra)structures that not only "guided behavior", but which also changed while they were being used; concepts of paths and traces, memory and actuality were derived from materials like polymers, rubber and sand... No one proposed having images of a beach on the wall, or decorating a website with bikinis, or

painting the walls in a restaurant purple to have the right setting for a perfect dinner...

MICHAEL HENSEL: Toyo Ito's Tower of Wind can be described as an existing example of an interdependent integration of architecture and media. The layered and translucent volume of the tower serves as a ventilation system. The data stream resulting from the environmental variables of the air stream, i.e. velocity, temperature and the like, is transferred into a complex lighting system. The issued ambient effects of both material translucence as well as the data stream issued by the complex, ongoing play of the lighting system cannot be divided into architectural and media effects, since both are mediated and submerged. In the near future, architecture and media will be able to be integrated in one surface/spatial compound. Advanced materials like synthetics and composites deliver the potential. Textile-like woven matrixes already serve as structural reinforcement for these new materials. Synthetics and composite materials with microtechnology embedded in the strands of their fiber reinforcement make intelligent material systems, within which the matrixes can distribute data and establish

immediate material re/activity.

NICK WEST: From both sides, the initial examples of convergence between media and architecture seem gimmicky: new media with simplistic "architecture" pasted on, or architecture with "new media" pasted on. From the new media side, the various attempts at creating 3D virtual worlds (Alphaworlds, Black Sun, VRML) have pointed toward the possibilities of convergence without offering a compelling reason for viewers to stick around and watch. From the architectural side, the obvious examples are those buildings and installations which have begun to incorporate a media "layer" as part of their design: the Tower of Winds, Times Square, Piccadilly Circus, Las Vegas, and any theme park. Not as obvious are examples like the newly "wired" spaces (like 55 Broad Street in Manhattan, or apartment buildings with T1 lines), and the various incarnations of "smart" houses. Chances are that this convergence "gimmick" will deepen and grow as it becomes necessary instead of merely clever. The creation, for example, of systems to provide constantly available caches of Internet material via satellite will create a supply

78

Everything which has to do with the physical aspects of architecture has traditionally been summed up in the term "tectonics". Tectonics is not only limited to construction, but includes a construction's covering as well. And last but not least, tectonics has to do with the way a building is built, the meaning of its parts and the mood that the architecture invokes. In the previous century, Architect Gottfried Semper developed the theory of the "Stoffwechselthese" in which the covering of the architecture, its skin, played an important role. Semper attributed architecture's origins to the satisfaction of the very first needs: the protection of the skin by another skin, fur or bark. He called this the "Prinzip der Bekleidung". All other forms of covering developed from this: the hand-woven rug and the woven cloth, but also the glazing of tiles, stucco work, the bronze-riveted wood sculpture of the Greeks, lacquering, mosaics and wallpaper. The development of textural origins into architecture then proceeded, according to Semper's "Stoffwechselthese", by means of a permanent metamorphosis from one material into another: wickerwork became textile, wood became stone, ceramics became metal. According to Semper, however, the echo of the textural origins always remained present, for example in the German words "Wand" ("wall") and "Zaum" ("bridle"), which resonate with "Gewand" ("gown") and "Saum" ("hem"). In his essay "Das Prinzip der Bekleidung", Adolf Loos emphasizes that for the

architect, Semper's theory means that he should, in making a design, always begin with the desired effect of the spaces he wants to produce in the sense of meaning and atmosphere. Secondly, he should look for a skeleton that has to carry the whole. In regard to the former, all different kinds of supplemental technologies have been increasingly taking over the roll of architecture's materiality in terms of the production of comfort and atmosphere. Some examples that spring to mind are air conditioning, artificial light, and (background) music. These technologies have now become inextricably connected with architecture, and the architect uses many specialized advisors in these areas while making a design.

The theories of Semper and Loos, however, are particularly interesting if we fully consider the role the media may come to play in architecture. For example, the step from wallpaper via photo-wallpaper to projection screen is, after all, not so extreme; it's no greater than the step from symbolic sculptures and chiseled inscriptions to billboards. The question is therefore to what degree media (will) comprise a natural part of architecture's tectonics. In your opinion, to what degree is it probable or even necessary that architects will, within the foreseeable future, call in help from specialized media consultants? And what would these media consultants be able to advise them about (even regardless of mov-

of immanent, permanent information - an architectural attribute.

LARS SPUYBROEK: On tectonics and textile: infrastructure and fabric should not be in the tectonic opposition of floor and wall/window. Every time, there is the underlying notion that feet are active and eyes are receptive. THIS IS DEAD WRONG. I think it was Ernst Junger who said that the infosphere was "the electronic dress of the world", which is rather MacLuhanian, but I would agree that every network is a constant extension of the skin, of action, of the sphere of action, without any (optical) depth of vision and perspective.

ing wallpaper)? What consequences will this ultimately have for the manifestation of architecture?

DICK RIJKEN: From a media perspective, a number of angles can be of interest: presentation (what can be seen or heard?), control (how to manipulate certain characteristics of the environment?), and infrastructure (for content as well as for control).

Research in display screen technology offers amazing vistas: right now, research labs are playing with flat and flexible display screens with image resolutions that are finer than the human eye can see and without any limit to their physical size (unlike TVs or current LCD displays). Imagine what this can do for architecture: walls full of dynamic displays (once that happens, we'll watch Robocop together)... On the other hand, where do we find photographic wallpaper nowadays? Will dynamic content make the big difference? Currently, background pictures on computer screens are referred to as 'wallpaper', soon our wallpaper itself will be a computer screen.

Also, all your examples (climate, lighting, sound) are becoming more and more computer-controlled: smart buildings, smart homes, etc. This raises the control issue: how to influence (tectonic) characteristics and behaviours of the physical environment? When does a room heat up, and how fast? How do I instruct my house? This ranges from occasional configuration (with the thermostat as a simple example) to direct interaction (real time control of certain parameters). Philippe Wegner (in his Philips days) worked at user interfaces for intelligent buildings. One of his designs was a 'magic wand' kind of pointer object: you pointed the device at the object you wanted to control (lights, sound sources, ventilators, etc.) in order to change its settings. Here as well, the dynamic aspect of these new technologies seems to be the most interesting. If a building has a very smart climate control system, can that have an effect on the size of its windows? A building's tectonic properties can be subject to constant change. This will not leave the physical design. Is the way my house talks to me over the phone part of its tectonics? I wonder what will happen when 'behaviour' becomes a standard part of the tectonic repertoire... It seems to me that in Lars Spuybroek's pavillion it already is.

I would put my money on portable (or 'hangable') displays, physically separated from but in communication with (portable) input devices like pointers, pens or microphones for speech input. If there is one thing we can predict, it is that these presentation and control technologies will develop further and further. Therefore, it may not always be a good idea to integrate them with physical structures in

NICK WEST: Media is continually dematerializing space by focusing our attention away from our physical surroundings. As a greater percentage of our lives becomes involved in these media flows, architecture will necessarily have to rethink its assumptions on how we interact with physical space. The obvious answer to the challenge will be to co-opt the media monopoly by actually incorporating media into the design of physical space. Instead of a competition between an increasingly less populated physical world and an ever-greater number of people clustered around their media viewers, why not eliminate the dichotomy altogether? What if the built environment could provide us with all the information that specialized viewers provide today? This addition of layers of "virtual" architecture could lead to a new conception of cities as collections of informatic flows, but grounded in space.

very rigid ways. You don't want to plaster your current TV into the wall if you know there will be projectors or hangable flat screens in a couple of years. This seems to call for generic rather than specific physical structures. Architects will have to deal with (generic) media infrastructure more than with (specific) media design. What goes through the wires of a computer is not an architectural decision, but the wires themselves need space, just like other infrastructural systems. Maybe this again takes us back to our discussion about context-dependent design, about which we now almost can say that architects' designs are contexts for media designs that are designed specifically for these contexts .

Anyway, all this does call for close collaboration between media designers and architects. Media and information technology consultants can talk with clients about expected media use and with architects about media and information infrastructures that support the expected media usage. And I do hope that these teams will come up with radically new concepts of what buildings are, once these are not just present in physical space only, but also extend themselves into different kinds of information environments. My house is no longer present in my street in my town, but also in my laptop and in my watch...

BART LOOTSMA: So far we have seen several instances of how media can influence the organization of architecture. Thus it seems possible to accept a more complex and cluttered form of urban planning because people could, via satellite navigation systems coupled with maps stored in a computer, be given directions in a manner that would still be efficient. The system of flyers used by groups who organize techno parties informs music and dance subcultures about where they need to be at a particular moment if they want to find something to their liking, much like the Spartacus guide does for homosexuals. This could allow otherwise "normal" places or buildings to have a very specific program at given moments (and thus not all the time). Just-in-time production and global tracking systems, for example like those which Rotterdam's harbor authority wants to organize globally for shipping traffic, diminish the need for large stock supplies and silos. Air traffic has long been inconceivable without a central air traffic control system, and this system will become even more optimized in the years to come. Do you see even more far-reaching perspectives in this area during the upcoming years in the way that the media will change the organization of architecture and urban planning? And can you also imagine specialized media consultants in the areas of urban and town planning? What will they be occupied with?

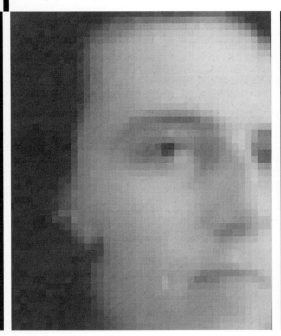

MICHAEL HENSEL: Architecture and media are both strong shapers of environments. If both shapers work in synergy towards an integrated product, contemporary urbanism may find its chance to maintain a large degree of organizational coherence and navigability instead of being segregated via endless fragmentation. Architects and media designers both work through the instrumentalization of graphic space. For media designers, graphic space serves to establish new types of information organization and distribution. Architects instrumentalize graphic space to be transferred into actual space. The different ways of working through graphic spaces may serve to stimulate new thought and new products for both disciplines.

WINY MAAS: I see two areas where you can find the influence of architecture on media: on one hand in the world of massiveness or the world of quantities, and on the other hand in the world of the individual. When you compare media to urbanism, you see that media generally deals with quantity, with a massive number of viewers or interpreters. This massiveness of people is a very fluid matter, because it has hypes, trends, and reacts as a kind of economy. It would be very thought-provoking to compare that to urbanism, because people tend to think of urbanism as very heavy and slow and as something you can't change easily. But when you consider parts of our horizon as becoming increasingly fast, you could also see it as a kind of urban matter, with trends and ups and downs. That notion makes it conceivable that parts of our society can be changed more easily. Of course it will take a lot of energy to make this work, because the matter in urbanism is much more slow than the matter in the world of media. The second notion from the world of media that I find interesting is the relationship between the individual and the media. Media changes the idea of space, for example when our intimacies are mixed with being in public spaces. This means that we're making another kind of environment. Does this development mean that our houses can be smaller, or that we will open our windows even more? Is it therefore logical to have smaller streets? Does it become conceivable that we should get rid of some of the borders between the private and the public as well, including physical borders? Or does it have the reverse effects? When you see media as a world of possible meetings, be they virtual or real, this might give architecture a model of rethinking public spaces.

DICK RIJKEN: Your examples are excellent illustrations of the way information (technology) transforms the way we deal with our physical environment. Developments like Just-in-time production will radically transform the transportation, storage and presentation of goods. What we are seeing right now is a very general trend of chain reversal: products are not made and then sold, but they are sold first, and then made. This results in micro-distribution infrastructures with, indeed, little need for large storage spaces, but also in different retail concepts. Selling a product is becoming an information-based activity, where the options you have initially exist in information rather than in matter. There may be one or two example products in a store, but they are rarely sold as-is. Once you have decided what you want and agreed to purchase, a packet of information is sent to a factory and the product gets made and shipped. Oddly enough, this means that you can't walk into a store and take the product home, but you do have much greater influence on the actual end result. What does this mean for the design of retail stores and shopping malls? At this moment, expectations are that this will result in opposite trends: day-to-day products like groceries will find their way to customers through electronic shopping lists and delivery services (there wasn't a lot of fun in grabbing a bottle of milk from a shelf in the first place), and luxury items will be presented in information and entertainment-rich environments (virtual as well as physical). Disney is becoming a shopping mall and shopping malls are becoming theme parks.

There are fully automated parking garages that can physically shuffle cars around, thus creating room for more cars than usual. Also, there are electronic signs all over the city that indicate the amounts of free spaces in the different parking garages. If we know exactly who needs to go from where to where, we can use less buses and trains. With regard to the organisation of space, 'feedback' is the key word. Traffic information is a well known example of providing feedback that drivers use to decide which route to take. There will be feedback about everything. Functional activities will become even more functional, based on real time information (as opposed to leisure activities, that will become more unpredictable and surprising). And again, timing is everything. The most dramatic impact of media will come from dynamic, real time information access. Information-rich transportation infrastructures will have a strong impact on mobility in urban environments. The Dutch Railway Company (NS) is currently investigating a new approach to their information infrastructure that is based on real-time coordination rather than on planning in advance.

Media consultants will work with architects, urban planners, policy makers, and other professionals and design information (infra)structures and interfaces that

BRUNO FELIX: Many activities that are still bound to a particular place as a result of being fixed to a particular infrastructure or facility are becoming increasingly mobile and increasingly capable of distribution using the possibilities offered by information technology. When broadcasting, education, a home for the elderly or a hospital can be present in any place at any time, they can not only make their services more efficient, but can also expand and deepen these services. Elderly people who can no longer live on their own but who can call for help at any moment, or teaching which takes place outside of the classroom, or a broadcasting organization that advises me about what films can be seen during a festival – these are no longer distant prospects. It will become more interesting when these kinds of institutes also begin to use each others' services. When these kinds of hybrids begin to appear, there will also be other demands placed on the constructed environment and on the way people move through this environment. With high school students and elderly people discussing the graying of the Netherlands in a forum facilitated by VPRO media, I begin to wonder if a classroom with three computers is really the most suitable place for such a discussion.

PHILIPPE WEGNER: In personal spaces, I don't see a merging of media and architecture happening yet. There are hardly any examples of the physical environment really supporting the use of electronic media, or of the electronic media being designed to make use of specific qualities of the environment. But it's important for the disciplines to start working together, because there are huge gaps between the two worlds, while people are using both and living in both. In the near future, I hope the two disciplines can merge in those semi-public/semi-private places where people meet in large numbers or for specific kinds of information, like bank offices and train stations. The places where you can already find this merging are in environments which have been expressly set up, like the Holocaust museum in California. In this museum, the environment in which electronic media was being used truly supported the intensity of the media.

WINY MAAS: It's conceivable that architecture will transform the media. When societies change, the physical surroundings change as well, and that will cause other demands for media. For example, in a very compact world, the issue of routing will become more important. So everybody might

allow for new ways of using (and creating) space. In these applications, I foresee a strong role for location-specific media (we were talking about them a while back). Moreover, these teams will come up with new concepts about urban identity. What is a city? A physical environment? An information environment? A way of thinking? A culture? Can I live in Rotterdam, even if I sleep in Utrecht?

BART LOOTSMA: Media also create independent spaces with boundaries and completely unique characteristics in a way that architecture would never be able to do. We have, for example, already discussed local radio stations, but we can also consider cable networks for television and telecommunications. Air traffic control defines corridors in the air which are invisible to the eye. Can you think of any other examples of spaces like these?

DICK RIJKEN: How about the bracelets that are used to imprison inmates inside their own homes? The bracelet cannot be taken off, and, as soon as the inmate leaves the house, it signals this event to headquarters. They can run, but they cannot hide. Also, there are experiments in the Netherlands that aim at regulating traffic flow through communication between a vehicle and the road: the road takes care of itself by controlling speed and distance between vehicles. In a

more mundane setting, mobile phone users can find their way through physical space by means of guidance in their ears from friends.

Actually, I think the most interesting issue may not be the fact that information can create space at all (a simple traffic light already does this, essentially), but that current and future media can do so in a very dynamic and ephemeral way. A while ago I witnessed some kind of convoy through the heart of Amsterdam: a couple of fancy limousines accompanied by police on motorcycles. Four motorcycles would block an intersection to provide smooth crossing for the limousines, while four others were already on their way to the next intersection. The limousines moved uninterruptedly through the heart of Amsterdam at some 60 km/h (what a dream). This is very similar to the flight traffic control example, and the elegance is in its temporary character. The normal (non-)flow of traffic was interrupted for only two minutes or so. Now there was obvious information involved (cops on motorbikes signaling drivers to stop as physical information sources), but it made me wonder whether the same kind of ephemeral effect can be achieved through very localised media (in time as well as in space) such as mobile phones or location-sensitive personal displays. Which, again, takes us back to our discussion about places as filters for information. There's more to it than meets the eye through weird spectacles that make you look like Robocop...

have a watch that will not only tell him the time, but also his location. I can see this kind of media happening in a kind of super-compact town. Imagine the city becoming dispersed, for example when people work more at home and are totally isolated from the world, seeing as they are in their own individual homes. This almost Norwegian society would prompt the issue if we were to lean more via the electronic media than we do now. Maybe we will look for other kinds of sensations, like tactile sensations, smell, maybe even virtual parks or journeys. This would accelerate those parts of the media which are still in an embryonic stage now.

NICK WEST: As the universally available bandwidth for media access increases, media will begin to acquire the persistence normally associated with the built environment. Currently, media are usually ephemeral: a show or a program or a daily newspaper has a certain time window during which access is available. More and more, both on the Internet and within cable systems, these media are becoming available on-demand: at the convenience of the viewer instead of being based on a previously determined schedule. But future developments in high-bandwidth individual access (always on), and high-bandwidth satellite caches of most media material (always on) point to a different future entirely: one in which media is a persistent, constantly accessible flow - more like a river than the on-and-off transmissions of radio and TV.

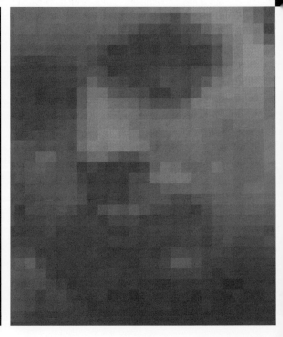

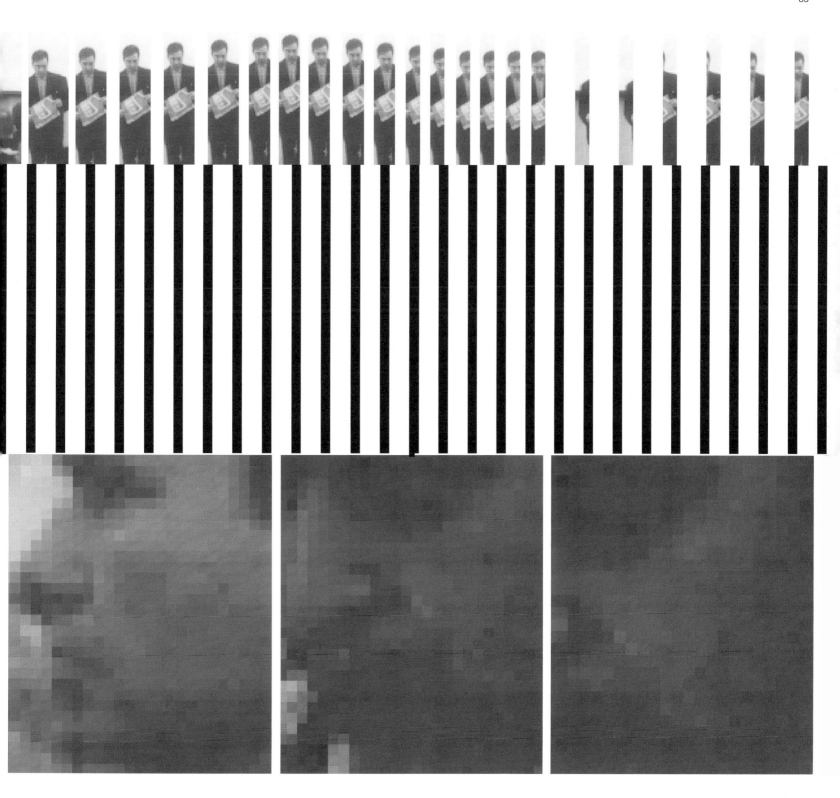

MEDIA AND ARCHITECTURE / ROELOF KIERS MASTERCLASS

COLOPHON

AUTHORS:
BART LOOTSMA AND DICK RIJKEN

COMMENTS:
BRUNO FELIX, MICHAEL HENSEL, BART LOOTSMA, GREG LYNN, WINY MAAS, BERT MULDER,
DICK RIJKEN, LARS SPUYBROEK, PHILIPPE WEGNER, NICK WEST

EDITORS:
EWOUT DORMAN AND MICHELLE PROVOOST (CRIMSON)

EDITORIAL BOARD:
MARIJKE BEEK, BRUNO FELIX, BART LOOTSMA, DICK RIJKEN

GRAPHIC DESIGN:
MIEKE GERRITZEN

TRANSLATION:
DOUGLAS HEINGARTNER

VIDEO STILLS:
HENRYK GAJEWSKI

PHOTOS:
GERTJAN KUIPER, BART LOOTSMA, MICK MORSSINK, FRANS SCHELLEKENS

ORGANIZATION:
PETRA SCHREVELIUS, MARJOLIJN BRONKHUYZEN

PRINTED BY DRUKKERIJ SSP AMSTERDAM

PUBLISHER:
VPRO AND THE BERLAGE INSTITUTE AMSTERDAM

ISBN:
90-6727-030-X

© VPRO AND THE BERLAGE INSTITUTE AMSTERDAM, 1998

THIS PUBLICATION IS A COLLABORATION BETWEEN THE VPRO AND THE BERLAGE INSTITUTE AMSTERDAM. IT WAS MADE POSSIBLE
BY THE FINANCIAL SUPPORT OF 'HET STIMULERINGSFONDS VOOR ARCHITECTUUR' (NETHERLANDS ARCHITECTURE FUND)